God Speaks
in
Many Ways

RUBY HARRIS

WESTBOW
PRESS®
A DIVISION OF THOMAS NELSON
& ZONDERVAN

WestBow Press books may be ordered through booksellers or by contacting:

WestBow Press
A Division of Thomas Nelson & Zondervan
1663 Liberty Drive
Bloomington, IN 47403
www.westbowpress.com
1 (866) 928-1240

ISBN: 978-1-4908-8017-4 (sc)

Library of Congress Control Number: 2015907434

Print information available on the last page.

WestBow Press rev. date: 07/17/2015

PREFACE

*I*n 1984 I gave up something I really loved because God let me know He had another direction for me to go. That is when I began to write poems not even realizing at the time what for. When I was in school, I could not make two words rhyme and now all of a sudden everything was making a poem.

I have been writing since and I have realized that it is God teaching me about life, problems, trials, pain, rejection and anything else that comes at me that could ruin my life if I didn't know God. His Word is so powerful and full of answers for every need we have. He has taught me to hide His Word in my heart that I might not sin against Him.

He has also taught me to hide His Word in my heart to recall it and be able to speak it over any problem, circumstance or frantic situation at any moment in my life. The power of God's Word is unfathomable until you realize that it is Total Truth and if you believe it and speak it to God when asking for help it can't be stopped. It is the means of keeping you connected to Him to understand when you just simply need to stop and spend time with Him and send praise straight to Him for a time of fellowship and worship.

I felt very impressed to add a scripture to each poem in this book hoping it will cause the reader to look it up and see the truth and power of God's Word. It hopefully relates in a way that verifies that all of this is God's plan and that He is speaking to us in many ways.

DEDICATION

This book is dedicated to all those readers who have experienced one of my poems and has been blessed. Also, To those who have responded with words of encouragement and hope that one day they will be circulated in a bigger way and reach more people that they too may be encouraged.

Praises to my Heavenly Father for loving me enough to let me live the lessons and be changed to become a willing vessel to be used by HIM.

IF GOD SAYS

If God says yes, can man say no?
If God says live, you must grow!
If God says blessed, how can you not be?
If God is your freedom, then you must be free!
If God says share, then you must let go!
If God says to know Him, then Him you must know
if God says peace, then you must not fear
If God says hope, He is always near
if God says joy, that makes you strong
If God says truth, He will never lead you wrong
If God says success, then you will rise
If God says see, then He will open your eyes
If God says hear, He will anoint your ears
If God says be happy, He will dry your tears
If God says stand, Then you will not fall
If God says surrender, then you give Him your all
If God says to witness He will give you His Word
If God says awaken, His alarm will be heard
If God says trust, He will never fail
If God says obey, you obey Him well
If God says dine, you come to His table
If God says healed, you know He is able
If God says look, then look at the SON
If God says Jesus, then He is the ONE
If God says come, He means to the cross
If God says victory, then know there is no loss
If God says mercy, then He wants us to forgive
If God says compassion, then we show how we live
If God says love, the example He will be
If God says child, then He is talking to me

Acts 18:10

How Many Ways Does God Speak

God can use some really weird things
To get your attention when He wants to speak
From the things that seem way too strong
To the things that are so weak
He can use just a brush of air
That gently blows past your skin
Or a leaf fallen from a tree
Or the bare limb where the leaf had been
He can use a spoken word
That before would have been ignored
In the quiet of night from a strangers mouth
Or from your heart where His word is stored
He can use a simple smile
For a tremendous way to communicate
That He has some news for you
In His time, He is never late
A twinkling star hanging in the sky
Can tell you much that God would say
How His power stays strong and true
For any problem in your day
The world is full of wonderful things
That speak to us of love so true
God just loves to take the time
To make them all speak to me and you
LISTEN!

lUKE 2:9

WHEN GOD IS IN THE MIDST

WHEN GOD IS IN THE MIDST
WHAT MORE COULD YOU ASK FOR
HIS PRESENCE IS SURROUNDING COMPLETELY
YOU DON'T HAVE TO WORRY ABOUT ANY WAR

WHEN GOD IS IN THE MIDST
WORRY HAS NO PLACE TO STAY
THAT IS WHY IT'S SO IMPORTANT
TO INVITE HIM INTO EVERY DAY

WHEN GOD IS IN THE MIDST
EVIL HAS TO RUN
FOR GOD BEING IN THE MIDST
BRINGS FELLOWSHIP RIGHT FROM HIS SON

WHEN GOD IS IN THE MIDST
YOU HAVE NO REASON TO FEAR
WHAT EVER TRIES TO MAKE YOU AFRAID
IS CONQUERED WHEN HE SAYS "I AM HERE"

WHEN GOD IS IN THE MIDST
I AM AWARE OF ALL HE HAS SENT
BEING SURROUNDED BY HIS MIGHTY SPIRIT
IS WHY I REST SO CONTENT

WHEN GOD IS IN THE MIDST
YOUR HOPE WILL NEVER DIM
KNOWING HE IS STANDING WITH YOU
KEEPS YOU CONNECTED TO HIM

WHEN GOD IS IN THE MIDST
HIS POWER FLOODS EVERY SITUATION
EVEN WHEN THINGS TRY TO "SLIP UP ON US"
HE IS AWARE OF ALL HIS CREATION

Genesis 1:1

GOD ALWAYS ENDS THE FIGHT

I KNOW THAT I AM DOING WHAT'S RIGHT
WHEN EVIL CONSTANTLY WANTS TO START A FIGHT.
I HEAR GOD'S VOICE AND MOVE TO OBEY
HERE HE COMES TRYING TO RUIN MY DAY.

I GET SIDE TRACKED AND LOSE MY THOUGHT
BUT, THEN GET BACK TO THE MESSAGE GOD BROUGHT
I MAKE A DECISION TO LET NOTHING DETER MORE
FOR I AM ANXIOUS TO SEE WHAT GOD HAS IN STORE.

HE ALLOWS THE SITUATION HANDED OVER TO ME
WATCHING LIKE A SHEPHERD FOR WHAT HE WILL SEE
I GET INVOLVED SEEING WHAT HE WANTS ME TO DO
I WILL GET IT TOGETHER AND FOLLOW IT THROUGH

GOD PROVIDES WHAT I NEED AND WAITS TO SEE
WHAT I WILL GET DONE WITH WHAT HE HAS GIVEN TO ME.
HE HAS A PLAN ALWAYS WITH PURPOSE TRUE
WHEN HE GETS IT STARTED, HE WILL STAY WITH YOU

DON'T BE AFRAID AND LET COURAGE PREVAIL
THERE WILL ALWAYS BE A STORY TO TELL
OF THE AWESOMENESS OF GOD AND FAITHFULLNESS GREAT
HE WILL SEND SO MUCH POWER IT WILL NEVER ABATE

GOD KNOWS OUR NERVES CAN BECOME FRAYED
WHEN WE HAVE STOOD UP AND HIS WILL OBEYED
WHEN EVIL COMES AND ARGUES ABOUT WHAT IS RIGHT
GOD SIMPLY SAYS "CHILD, I HAVE THIS FIGHT"

II Chronicles 20:15

THE POWER OF GOD'S NAME

I have no one
But myself to blame
For not using the power
Given in God's Holy Name
I just sit at ease
And let things go awry
Until my whole being
Wants to scream and cry
At some point in the misery
That has managed to abound
God reminds me of all the times
Of power in His Name that I have found
I then have to repent
Of the lost time I have endured
When there could have been victory
He has constantly assured
There is power available
That He has made all mine
I have to go to the source
Before the need I find
I must start my day right
I just have to look above
Commune with my Father
Get absorbed in His love
Then the time that I need Him
When all has gone awry
I can live in His power
Without a need to cry

Acts 4:12

WHERE IS YOUR HAMMER?

When you try to determine
Just which sin is the worst
You should take time to remember
What Jesus said in one verse

We all have sinned and come short
We all had hammer and nail in hand
Just as though we were at the cross
Nailing our sins along with the whole land

Some took longer than others
Some thought the nail not big enough
It may not be able to hold the "big sin"
Driving through this wood so rough

Those who didn't have so many to nail
Picked out ones they thought needed help
Offering to drive the nail for them
After all that's a pretty hard step

We don't need help with our sins
When to God we really want to give
The whole batch of our sin at once
For the life He has promised we can live

We want to be forgiven by the Father
We want to be clean and pure
But, we tend to think we need to remind others
Their guilt will forever endure

We need to surrender the hammer and nails
The price is fully paid
You will quit arguing which sin is the worst
When the hammer is at the cross laid

John 19:18

ONLY GOD CAN

My feeling are once again trying to take control
Wanting to take away God's peace in my soul
I Won't Let It

Too many thoughts bouncing around in my head
Giving me too many things to dread
I Won't Let it

Too many things with which to deal
Not wanting my emotions to calm down and heal
I Won't Let it

I and Me and My must get out of the way
Letting myself experience God's day
I Will Let it

My emotions and feelings I give to Him
Letting my day not be dreaded and grim
I Will Do it

Lord, let me let you turn my thoughts around
Put a smile on my face and take away this frown
I Will Let You do it

Let my will be what You desire
Walk me through the emotional flood and fire
Only You Can do it

Psalms 46

THINGS

God has been teaching me lessons
On the value of "things"
Worldly stuff we try to hold on to
How easily they can sprout wings
One moment you have them in hand
The next moment they are gone
You can be totally surrounded by "things"
The next moment you can stand alone
We must be choosy about these "things"
What it is we try to hold as ours
The enemy named Evil can control us
For "things" have some hidden powers
They can control our behavior
Especially if someone begins to show a desire
To have those "things" we hold so dear
How to get them, they begin to inquire
"Things" can change our focus
They can control our total view
Eveybody except ourselves can be blocked out
Controlling what we for others do
I don't want to be in the control
Of "things" that will not forever last
God help me to let go of temporary stuff
The "things" that are eternal, Hold them fast

Matthew 1:21 AND John 3:16

NORMAL DAYS

On those days when you find yourself wanting
Things to become as normal as they used to be
Do you find yourself wondering at all
Exactly what "normal" in your day would see?

"Normal" could be a job you don't like
Or it could be a pile of bills to pay
Normal sometimes is not at all what we want
It just seems the thing we need to say

Have you ever thought what "normal" really is?
Boredom could be the word to best describe
Change is what we all seem afraid of
A dull routine keeps us better satisfied

Just maybe God in all His wisdom
Allows "normal" to sometimes go its own way
To keep us apprised of His hand in our life
And letting us know He wants in our day

He keeps us from getting in a rut
That "normal" will deepen and bore us to tears
We keep "normal" hanging around all the time
For we are too comfortable with our worries and fears

I want God to do away with "Normal"
Replace it with the kind of day He gives to me
Maybe "supernatural" would be just the type of word
To rule my day and keep me "normal" free

Psalms 122:7

SUPPOSE

Suppose God came to visit and ask me
If I was willing to trust Him in a way
That would require total commitment on my part
And His every word I would obey
Would I have to think about it?
Would I have to suppose, This? or That?
Would I question Him forever about How?
And wonder if on my face I will fall flat?
Would I wonder if I would look like a fool?
As if God would lead me down that path
Would I be afraid to say no for fear
That my refusal would bring down His wrath?
Would He even want to continue to ask
When all my questioning was done?
Would He reconsider His choice of me
And decide I was not the one?
Would I be able to skip all the questions?
Could I answer without even a guess?
Could I look at Him and His request consider
Trusting Him enough to simply say, YES!

II Chronicles 20:20

GOD IS ALWAYS DUE OUR PRAISE

Lord, I thank you for the morning
Letting me see the sunrise
Thank You for all the beauty
You let me see through these eyes
I thank You for the sunshine
I thank You for the rain
I thank You for the lessons
You teach me through my pain
I thank You for the birds singing
Beautiful songs that I can hear
Thank You for reminding me
In all things that You are near
I thank You for Your blessings
For Your mercy and Your peace
Thank You for Your strength and joy
For Your compassions that never cease
Thank You for friends that love me
For smiles that replace my frowns
For Your Spirit that abides in me
Through all lifes ups and downs
Thank You for my family
Reminding me of unconditional love
Speaking volumes to me time and again
Of my wonderful, Heavenly Father above
Thank You for reminding me
That all I have comes from You
And no matter how much I thank You
There's always more praise that You are due

Revelation 19:5

USING GOD'S GRACE

When God was feeding the children of Israel
Manna from Heaven to sustain each day
They were allowed to gather just enough to get by
Anything more would ruin and waste away

The day before the Sabbath each week
They were allowed to gather for two days and yet
God warned them about trying to store up
More than they were allowed to get

God gives us of His grace
In much the very same way
He wants us to not worry about tomorrow
It causes us to waste His grace for today

I need too much of God's grace for today
To let worry take any away from tomorrow
If I don't use what God gives me for right now
I could face my next day with a load of sorrow

God knows what we will face
On every future day He allows
Without that amount of grace He supplies
We will drown in Why's? When's? How's?

I have decided that I will trust Him
I don't want worry to have any part of my day
Knowing His grace is fully sufficient
Makes it easy to believe every word He has to say

Genesis 22:8

WHAT IS GOD UP TO

Have you ever watched something unusual
Trying to figure out what it was going to do?
Every day you looked at it another time
But, not much change was it going through

You get kind of tired of the watching
You want to see something develop soon
But, day after day nothing seems to take place
You wonder if the thing will ever bloom

I guess I just gave it away
Yes, even though we thought it a useless weed
But, now it has bloomed so pretty
We are talking of saving the seed

We almost pulled it up to discard
The waiting was causing our nerves to stress
But, if we had given in to the destruction
What it was, we would always guess

Don't we so get tired of waiting on God?
Wondering what it is He wants to do
We want to do some "weeding" of our own
Not giving Him time to get through

God does things in His own time
He wants to bless us with beauty rare
If we keep pulling up what he has planted
There will never be any beauty there

I know better than anyone else
it is better to allow anxiety to abate
For if we allow God His time to work
The beauty will be worth the wait

Ecc 3:11

No Earthly Reason to Whine

Lord, don't let me a whiner be
For it would waste all Your mercy I see
Your grace that daily, on me, You bestow
Let's me see all the goodness You show
You give me love and many friends
Along with Your compassion that never ends
In the middle of the hard times and pain
Your hands hold me time and again
You find ways to let me see You
In everything that I have to go through
It makes the suffering seem so much less
Because Your faithfulness is never a guess
What a Father to love this child so
So much from Yourself, You willingly bestow
You gave Your Son to make life better for me
Trusting in His sacrifice keeps me so free
With all these wonderful blessings, I find
There is no earthly reason for me to whine

ISAIAH 26:3

WHY DO WE WORRY?

Why do we worry when God says not to do it?
We keep right on when He wants us to quit
He has provided a way for us not to have to
But, we spend a world of time wondering what to do

He shows us the flowers and the beautiful birds
We just seem to ignore all of His teaching words
He says we are more valuable than the both of them
We somehow seem not to believe Him

He said our name is written right in His palm
Should that not be enough to keep us quiet and calm?
He said He knew us before we were in the womb
But, yet we want to dwell on all the doom and gloom

He said He knit us together just like he drew the design
But, I still want to find fault with this body of mine
The world is full of people just like me
Never satisfied with what God wants me to see

We keep looking for things to worry about
All we accomplish is sinking deep in our doubt
I just know God is wondering why we do not obey
Can't we understand His love and live life His way?

When we start to sink to the point we will drown
Then we scream for God to reach His hand down
As He picks us up and sets us on a solid place
Worry should disappear with the covering of His grace

What will happen now that He has come to our rescue?
Will the lesson of the birds and flowers teach us what to do?
Is it enough to know our name is in the palm of His hand?
Will worry keep winning or will our faith in Him stand?

Matthew 10:31

ALL THOSE LITTLE THINGS

I got up this morning
Planning to spend time in God's Word
Just about the time I got it open
This is what I heard:
Why is that the chosen lesson?
That topic is not so important right now
I replied right back in my mind
I might need to help someone know how
Then the devil came right back
Saying look at your tattered fingernails
Are you going to work like that?
He gets really low when it seems all else fails
He kept reminding me about the time
I knew that I was doing well
I had put aside something else I would have done
Because someone, about Jesus, I might need to tell
Then the sorry creature reminded me
That I had a toe nail that was sore
Oh, the lengths to which he will go
to block me knowing all God has in store
All these silly little things
That can really wait another day
I need to take time to sit and listen
Let God tell me what He has to say

Matthew 28:18-20

TOUGH DAYS

The last two days have been really tough
But, I know God is changing me
He is helping me to react more His way
Not in the circumstances that I see
There have been some rough ones
I wanted to rant and scream and cry
I found myself wanting to yell at God
Asking, "What is the reason?" "Why?"
He began to show me some reasons
Before I had a chance to act so bad
There were a lot of questions on my part
But, all the answers, He had
He showed me how He was teaching me
Where I was not really depending on Him
People could really cause me some anguish
My focus was too much turned on them
I was getting a bit too anxious
Whether or not He was answering my pleas
I was asking for His help over and over
But, not exactly humble or on bended knees
I was not taking enough time
To get before Him and being still
I was trying to pray while doing something else
Which was totally the opposite of His perfect will
He gently spoke right to my heart
In a non- misunderstanding way
Telling me to look all around
I would find Him in every part of my day
He showed me He has already gone ahead
To open some doors where others are closed
Reminding me to continue my prayers
Seeing Him do things I would never have supposed

Matthew Chapter 5

A BLANK MIND

Have you ever felt that your mind went blank?
You couldn't put two thoughts together at all
You find yourself wondering if it will turn around
Or, are you getting a wake up call?
A lot of wrong thoughts sure find a way
To flood your mind in a flash
They will try to run you in circles with fear
Hoping to see you in one great crash
But, we must remember that Jesus has said
Most battles with evil will take place in our mind
He will do whatever it takes
To keep us searching for peace to find
If we fill our mind and our hearts
With God's Word before this kind of attack
We will have ammunition ready when bombarded
To begin straightway to fire right back
We must remember that any battle with evil
Is in God's hand to win
If we know how to use God's Word as a weapon
The victory will come time and time again

II Cor 10:4

LOOKING BEHIND WON'T FIND YOUR FUTURE

You can't find your future if you keep looking back
Turning your head so much will keep you off track
All you will see when you keep looking over your shoulder
Are the things left behind that can hit like a run away boulder
Things kind of run over you when you stop to look around
You must press onward if you are "future" bound
You don't need to mess with things left behind
Those things that keep on messing with your mind
They make you wonder and operate in fear
Making you feel alone where no one can hear
The person you are is ready to move on
But, looking behind can keep you from getting it done
The future is a funny kind of place to be
To get there and enjoy it you have to be free
You have to dump the load that has you burdened down
Take nothing to the future that will cause you a frown
Choose what you need and only take that part
Make sure it will be a great comfort to your heart
Take nothing from the past that will cause fear or pain
The future is the plaee for the right kind of gain
To live in the future in the right frame of mind
Be sure God's grace is the first thing that you find
Leave the past with its heartache and fear
Build a future on knowing that God is so near

Isaiah 43:18-19

GOD DOESN'T WORK LIKE YOU AND I

God doesn't work like you and I
Over the things that make us cry
When He sees the tears He knows where to start
To mend all things tearing at our heart
God knows what it takes to get our attention
In His Word a few times He did mention
That He would be our father and our mother
He would be a sister and a brother
He promised also that He would never leave
Even though it appears so when the world makes us grieve
Our emotions get so loud that we can't hear His voice
We cry more tears over the wrong choice
God doesn't work like you and I
We should go to Him first but we always try
To fix things ourselves and not bother Him
That is why our lives always stay so grim
God doesn't work like you and I
He will let us struggle and our own plans to try
Until we are broken and then our knees bend
Begging our Father, this heart pain to mend
God has promised peace that we can't understand
If we listen to Him then we won't have to demand
That He come running when things go awry
We won't have to panic and we won't have to cry
God has a plan and He knows we will object
Until the moment our lives are a wreck
He patiently waits until our rope has no knot
Then we run to Him for He is all we have got
God wants us to know that He is all we need
He talks to us constantly and we still won't heed
When our heart is breaking and we wonder why
Then we remember God doesn't work like you and I

Romans 8:28

God Clears up Boggled Minds

Oh, those things that boggle my mind
Making peace a hard commodity to find
Like a sandstorm swirling in my head
Causing monotony that I truly dread
Why do I let it get into my brain?
Causing me on occasion to feel utterly insane
Things are presented that are as noisy as a zoo
Keeping me wondering what next to do
On it goes like an unending song
Making even small things seem all wrong
The way to end the assualt of confusion
Keeping me free of dread and delusion
Think on the things that God has said
Let Him calm my heart and clear up my head
Stop the sandstorm with the debris flying
Stop listening to evil and all of his lying
Realize God is truth and He will set me free
Let Him do the talking which allows me to see
Wherein lies the power that He alone does possess
What my mind is filled with I don't have to guess
God is the answer and He alone can cause me
To dwell on His good thoughts and live trouble free
If I listen to Him and obey His will
My boggled mind will be totally peaceful and still

Isaiah 26:3

WAYS TO PRAISE

I was just thinking this morning
About some new and powerful ways
To send to God, our Heavenly Father
Some adoring and wonderful praise
He has truly been so faithful
To take care of needs of mine
That I needed more than "ordinary" ways
To praise Him for intervention divine
It didn't take long to see
That old ways were worship tools too
They were just the ways I have available
For what I needed to do
There was a song already in my heart
That I used to always sing
The words were perfect to tell Father, God
What joy His help to me will bring
I read to Him a word of scripture
That He had placed on my mind
It had given perfect peace to me
His great peace, He allowed me to find
I bowed my knees and head to Him
To whisper thanks for goodness and grace
He always sent me more than enough
When the enemy and I met face to face
I began to realize at that moment
My heart was filled with much praise
God didn't worry if they were new or old
He just wanted me to enjoy the ways

Isaiah 43:16

GOTTA KEEP THOSE EMOTIONS IN CHECK

Feelings aren't good witnessing tools
If they go bad and stand in the way
Of repentance and forgiveness to others
Who try so hard to ruin your day
We will all face times of adversity
When we want to take revenge on our own
But, God said that is not the way to do it
He didn't do it for His own Son
It sometimes seems so deserving
That we take matters unto our own
Whether we do or whether we don't
Seems like these feelings are never gone
Besides! It is our right to be "beside ourselves"
When we have so offended been
After all it has happened more than once
And probably will again
I will ask for a special gift from God
It is one I really do need
I need to be able to forgive without condition
I need to be able to sow good seed
I need to keep my feelings in check
To be able to help those in my path
It will work out so much better
If I don't give in to wrath
When I try to help someone understand
They are covered by God's great grace
It sure will help if it can be verified
By the sincerity of voice and smile on my face

Psalms 4:6-7a

MANAGING TIME

Time is really flying so fast
It's hard to know what to do
So much in one day needing done
There needs to be four of you

Too many things on my mind
There's not enough hours anymore
Not enough is getting done
But, my body is really tired and sore

I don't seem to have time for fun
By the time all the chores are through
It's past time to lay this body down
I am done till the sun again plays "peek-a-boo"

I can lay aside some things
Stuff that can be done another day
But, I can't ignore my time with God
For He shows me how to live His way

This is one thing I can't give up
For I would surely live in despair
When I go to God and speak with Him
I want to know He's always right there

He doesn't react to time like me
He moves continually at a steady pace
He knows I don't manage time very well
That's why He covers me with so much grace

Ecc 9:11-12

THINGS UNKNOWN

There are times in life that you don't know
What the days will hold for you
You can spend way too much time
Wondering how and what you will do
It can get really scary in the natural
Faith has to be the place you operate
Faith deals with the things unseen
With faith there is no debate
You either believe what God says
Depending on truth to come from His Word
Or wonder if that other voice is right
The one trying to make you react to what you heard
God did not send His Son for condemnation
Therefore evils voice is easy to recognize
It is the one that is trying to scare you senseless
Filling you up with Whats? And Whys?
God is the voice of comfort and love
He speaks in a voice that condemns us not
If we are listening and obeying His voice
It doesn't matter Where? or What?
We don't have to live in fear of things unknown
With God there is never a surprise
He knows all that we will go through
For God is watching through His own eyes
He tends to his "sheep" as careful as can be
His sheep know what voice they hear
If it is not the one they are familiar with
They know the enemy is somewhere near
The Father knows the enemy is there
I don't have to worry what is in store
For every path that He chooses for me
He has walked that way before

II Cor 5:7

Pain Killer For The Heart

When my heart is starting to break
Father, God knows what steps to take
To stop the explosion that is about to take place

When the pain gets in seemingly without end
He is the only one with power to mend
He starts flooding it with a ton of Grace

God has Grace that acts just like glue
Moving and repairing what the pain tries to do
It gets in places off limits to other things

Grace from God can get in the right place
Returning the smile pain took from your face
Make sure your heart continually sings

Pain is a weapon the enemy will use
Hurting you so quickly your mind to confuse
But, God has the ultimate pain reliever

He sends His peace that has no end
With understanding that He is truly a friend
The peace He promises to every believer

It's up to us if we let the pain win
We can let God's Grace prevent it getting in
He knows how the enemy to block

Let Him send grace and peace like a flood
Remember you are covered by Jesus' blood
He will let you stand as strong as THE ROCK!

Psalms 31:3

WATCH YOUR THINKING

Ever had a day when the master of evil
Tries to unleash self-pity on your mind
Wanting you convinced that no one cares
Telling you there is not one friend to find
He wants you to believe all is bad
That you can't win no matter what you do
Lies, lies, he's the master of lies
His kind of thinking can't possibly be true
One thing you must know about Evil
His kind of thinking keeps you down
Negative thoughts trying to rule your life
The kind of negative that would make God frown
God is wanting you to realize
That in anything, He can work for your good
When you think like God tells you to
Evil's lies can't touch you if he could
The secret to the right kind of thinking
Is to learn who is worthy of our trust
God is the one who speaks no lies
Evil's kind of thinking is a big bust
When he starts speaking all his lies
Remind yourself to stop up your ears
Don't let his garbage fill your mind
You will find God's peace replacing your fears
Begin your day with true worship and praise
To God who is watching over you and know
You then can tell the evil one what to do
Take his evil thought and go

I Cor 16:13

ANSWERS ABOUT TIME

I went to the Lord for help
With a problem not knowing just how
He would choose to help me
But, I told Him I needed it NOW

I didn't hear a reply from Him
So, I went back again
This time the question I ask
Was just simply, "When?"

I ask for some sign from Him
That He was hearing my plea
"Sufficient is my grace, my child"
His voice was reminding me

Still, I just had to have more
A stronger answer was my cry
Lord, things aren't changing fast enough
Could You tell me, Why?

The world seems to be getting worse
My situation is never changing, too
Even though provision comes for each day
Is there more I need to do?

Where in time will my time be
When I know Your blessing is great
When things will be so perfect
Joy and peace will never abate?

He said to me, "Oh, my precious child
You are filled with such worry and despair
You are missing your appointed time of rest
Over the fear that I am not there"

"You should have joy in abundance
Knowing you are a child of mine
Questions shouldn't need such pressing answers
Your faith should work well with my time"

Ecc 3:1

WHAT WOULD YOU DO?

What would you do if you didn't have God
To hold you up when things go wrong?
What if He didn't give you courage
When your courage was all but gone?
Just who do you think you could run to
To get the amount of help to get you through
When the world is collapsing all around you
And you know it's just God and you?
Sometimes friends are not the answer
For they cannot give of themselves anymore
They too have been drained by their own needs
They are asking God, their souls to restore
Talking about the problem
Is not a bad thing to do
If it's God that you are sharing with
For He has the time to talk with you
God has all the time that is needed
To listen and hear the need of your heart
You must remember that is where you need to go
Run to Him at the very start
So, What would you do if you didn't have God
When the cares of life are getting you down
If His hand wasn't extended right out to you
I am afraid my friend, you might just drown
Be very careful to be thankful
That God is aware in all that you do
If you are in trouble and running to Him
He, in turn, is headed straight to you

Luke 24:38-39

Jesus Blood Turns Black Sin White

It's amazing how much light a candle will produce
Chasing away darkness as swift as can be
Such a tiny flame but so productive
Just like one drop of Jesus' blood for me

That one drop cleansed me completely
It took no more, no less
Whether it did what it was intended or not
I know that I don't ever have to guess

God said He would send His Son
He would shed His blood for my sin
He also said that He cannot lie
If I believe I WILL be "born again"

I believe He gave Jesus as a gift to the world
He was crucified just like God had said
He did what was promised if I would believe
I know on that cross is where His blood was shed

The drop destined for me fell so free
It cleansed me from the blackness of sin
Lit my world with cascades of illumination
Just like a candle that burns within

Jesus is the reason for my well lit life
The red of His blood turned my black sin white
I should be burning just like that candle
Shining like the SON to help end someone's dark night

Revelation 1:5

GOD'S WONDERFUL PROVISIONS

In all the times that the devil throws things at us
Trying to make us think that God is slack
God sends far more to us to cause celebration
Than evil can conjure up to throw right back

God always sends enough to keep us thankful
Of all His mercies and compassions promised each day
He has a new batch ready with the morning sun
Dispersing them as needed as we walk His way

Sometimes it seems that too much comes at once
We have a bit of trouble finding that great blessing
But, God has promised that He has it ready
Believing His Word will keep us from guessing

He sends something happy to cover all the sad
Sometimes we have to focus the direction of our eyes
He has seen all that is coming our way
He will never be caught by surprise

You should never worry about how God provides
The great blessings that gives our faith a boost
We should be thankful for the forgiveness of sin
Things that has us bound from which we have been loosed

He has made a great provision that will keep us free
We have the privilege of living in the freedom of the cross
His provision will never get "lost in the shuffle"
His words, "Father forgive them", paid our security cost

Luke 23:34

How to Help God Out

It is so hard to be quiet
When you know someone has to learn
A lesson that only God can teach him
Even though your heart will yearn
To reach out and fix the things
That God says for you to let go
If you keep on trying to be a rescuer
Then God's power will not show
You will hinder what He is trying to do
For now He also had to deal with another
This is not one of those places your help is needed
Even though you think you are helping a brother
Your place is to be in prayer for the one
That is being dealt with by the Master
This is the only way that you will find
That an answer will come any faster
God has to move in His way and time
We will find that He knows the way
That will reach the heart of the wayward one
Only He knows the hour and the day
We have to stay content in His will
Keep our hands off the solution we want to see
For we will wind up being a temporary answer
God is seeking one good for all eternity

Genesis 18:14

LIKE A DEER PANTING FOR WATER

All of a sudden it seems there is something missing
My heart doesn't seem to beat like it should
It is filled with so many feelings all of a sudden
I feel like it's streaking like a deer through the wood
It's panting for air from the pressure it feels
Only stopping for a moment to listen for sound
Wondering if it could rest for a minute or two
Hiding in the cover of nature not wanting to be found
It's beating for a baby born so very small
Trying to send strength for it's own to be strong
At the same time for a friend that is battling cancer
Wishing with every beat that someone is wrong
It's hurting for a neighbor that is facing despair
For the love of her life has wounded her sore
Too, her health that may be bringing bad news
On her plate there is room for no more
It is trying to beat strong for people younger than I
Whose job on the morrow may not be
But. most of all trying to beat and keep me alive
For sadness is trying to drain the life out of me
I know that Jesus can handle it all
He has promised to do this for me
He has far more experience than I ever would
His heart melted in Him when He hung on that tree
I have taken my eyes off the One that is able
To take care of all those affecting my heart
Like a deer that has lay down to recover from the run
I can only rest if I quit trying to do His part

Psalms 22:19

THOU SHALT NOT LIVE ON EMOTIONS

Your emotions can batter, bruise and tear
Until you can wonder if God does care
Trying to make decisions so right
Can bring concern, winding you up tight
Then like an old clock no one will take
You're wound so tight all the springs break
In every direction the emotions begin to "fly"
No tears will come now, you can't even cry
How in the world can you ever mend
Bring all the parts together again?
Emotions are not meant your world to rule
For emotions will become the ultimate tool
That evil will use to tear you apart
Beating you up and breaking your heart
We need emotions to bring a good balance
But, emotions alone can't produce enough talents
To keep you productive and hold you in check
Wisdom and Sound thinking don't allow emotions to "wreck"
With God's help the three work together well
Bringing emotional healing that works without fail

James 1:5

ADDICTED TO HOPE

I find I am addicted to hope
Just as the Bible said to do
My hope has been my mainstay
For more years than a few
I am always hoping for the best
But, it seems the worst is what I get
But, when it comes right down to it
It's still hope that I am hoping for yet
The years have come and they have gone
I have seen results of hope come too
A few things that I have hoped the more for
They have seemed to not come through
The waiting has taken its toll on me
For it seems that hope I have not understood
For if you are living as though you have hope
Then hope would sustain you just like it should
If I am going to live as though I have hope
I have to know where my hope lies
When my hope is wearing me thin
I have to take a look through God's eyes
Hope does not have a time limit
It seems like it is a lot like love
When all else fails and nothing is happening
Hope can stop a lot of push and shove
If our hope is in God our Father
And the love He gave in Jesus, His Son
Then our hope is founded in the right place
Hope will bring us to our final "Well Done"

Romans 5:5

GOD'S VIRUS PROTECTION PROGRAM

It's great that the Holy Spirit
Has a 24-7 "virus detector"
It can pick up on every evil plot
Working like a secret deflector

Everytime you are in true worship
God turns the "virus detector" on
For in a moment, even in God's presence
Evil injects a thought and then makes it run

The "virus detector" is God's Holy Spirit
He knows when strange thoughts appear
He shoots His "lazer" to your heart
Letting you know the enemy is near

Then it's totally your decision
To block or allow it to come through
The "virus detector" works really, really well
But, the deleting action is up to you

Let the Holy Spirit do its alerting job
Respond like God has instructed you
Then you can go back to worshipping Him
Just like you had started to do

Psalms 95:6-7

Slow But Sure

I don't know how I can be so slow
In learning the lessons God has for me
Especially when it comes to laying my feelings aside
So that myself is from me free
I think I know so much sometimes
That God has to just back away
I keep on trying to figure it out
I can't hear what He has to say
He tries to show me His way
But, I can't get past "poor old me" for gain
Pain is something I don't like at all
I tend to push away what causes the pain
I have finally realized that I rejected
The very thing God used to teach me His plan
If I want to quit being so slow
I must yield myself into His hand
The speed with which God will then teach me
Might totally make my head want to spin
But, my heart will live in total peace
For God will have found a way to get in

Psalms 25:12

GOD'S GREAT GIFT OF PEACE

God gives many gifts to His children
We can truly argue which is the greater one
There is no argument that can stand
On the claim the best is God's Son

The other gifts that He gives to us
Like Joy, Grace and Wisdom great
Compliment all the others He sends
Presenting to us Peace that does not abate

No greater peace can be given
Than that which God, Himself will provide
When things come that want to rip us apart
We can go in His peace to hide

Trust is the great attribute
That leads to God's kind of peace
The world canot understand the miracle of it
God gives so much that it cannot cease

When you go to God when a problem comes
Ask Him to handle the situation for you
You can literally walk away with such peace
That you know He is faithful and true

Just to experience this great peace of God
When all your emotions know you should drown
Handing it over to Him and letting Him work
The confirmation arrives: God did not let you down

Eph 2:14

THE PROBLEM WITH DOUBT

The worst problem I have with doubt
Is having a problem that I can't figure out
When there are no answers that I can find
Doubt jumps in and really plagues my mind
I start to wonder and come up with a guess
How to fix things that are in such a mess
Every way I go my mind comes up blank
I wear myself out and realize my spirit sank
Sometimes sinking so far I start to lose hope
Making me feel that I am at the end of my rope
I know that it is God that comes to remind me
If I would ask, He would help me to see
That He has answers when nothing else will do
I don't have to wait for it to fall "out of the blue"
Why, when He promised I don't have to thirst
Did I not go to Him with it first?
So much frustration and anguish do I cause
When I don't go to Him and quietly pause
Asking His help so that I don't have to fret
Realizing that He has not refused me yet
I need to take a break and tell Him of my sorrow
For I went into time and tried to borrow
Worries that I had enough of today
When He has tried over and over to show me His way
I turned a minor problem into an earthquake
All I accomplished was my faith to shake
Doubt jumped on it and caused a great frown
Flooding with a vengeance that tried to drown
All hope that God had sent me today
Just because I couldn't fix it my way

James 1:6-8

JESUS CAN HANDLE IT ALL

When I am in a predicament
With things too many to handle
I feel like I am wandering in the dark
Till God suddenly lights me a candle
He knows that I am in trouble
Trying to find my way out
Nothing that I have tried is working
He's coming to my rescue no doubt
He knows I can't find an answer
For so far the answer is His alone
He hasn't shown me any final solution
The time for showing His plan will come
We really shouldn't get stressed out
When we feel like we can't see the way
God has given us His super strength
Renewing it every morning, day after day
Jesus gave us all He had
We shouldn't be afraid to give Him our trust
How many times has He come to our rescue?
How many times has He our fears hushed?
It doesn't matter what we can't handle
If on the Name of Jesus we call
For in His great plan of caring for His children
He gave Jesus authority to handle it all

John 14:14

WONDERING

The great God of the Universe
Is becoming so visible to me
So awesome and so enduring
His creation He is allowing me to see
All the wonder He has created
Things both great and small
What would cause a God so great
To bother with me at all
To knit together one such as I
Knowing me so far ahead of time
What could have been the reason
That I was on His mind
He took the time to plan for me
Maybe even before the world was formed
To place me in His reserved special place
Until the time came for me to be born
Into a world created just for me
The sun and the moon in place
His creation waiting He gave me life
He baptized me with His grace
He sent His Son to this same earth
Another miracle He had prepared
Giving His life to give me to His Father
Proving how much He truly cared
As I reflect on it all, His purpose for me
I could sit forever and His love ponder
But, He has instilled in this heart of mine
I am not here just to sit and wonder

John 12:27

WHISPERS FROM HEAVEN

God just loves to whisper
In His children's ear
"Don't forget for a moment
I am so very near"
"There's not a moment of any day
That I am not close by"
"I hear your every thought
Whether it's worship or a sigh"
"I love to hear the worship thoughts
For It makes my heart so glad"
"I also hear your worries and fears
Along with all that makes you sad"
"I feel your pain and suffering"
"You can come and cast your care"
"If you will come to worship
I will take more than my share"
"My children are so precious to me"
"Their very lives I will defend"
"Thoughts of worship open all of Heaven
Freeing the blessings I will send"
"Don't ever think I will forget
Where you are and what you're going through"
"When it gets so overwhelming
Let me tell you what to do"
"Come near too me and think "worship""
"Open your mouth and empty its praise"
"That is the key to the Holy Spirit
Whispering love into all your days

John 14:15

WALKING WITH GOD

I have walked with God down many roads
He has been so faithful to take over the loads
That the world has piled on me whether my fault or not
He is my answer to questions of How? When? and What?

As He has taken me over paths up and down
His constant peace has found a way to surround
My every move as advancement was made
No possession of mine could make any kind of trade

God's kind of gifts are so extraordinaire
They stay in a way to remind you that He is there
As the roads went through valleys and over each hill
I knew that I was walking in His divine will

He took me to places where He taught me to survive
No one had to remind me that my God was alive
He was with me when my life should have ended
He was there when doctors had a hand in me being mended

Every part of my life has been blessed with His touch
That is the reason I share these words so much
He gives me hope when nothing else will do
He wants me to share all these feelings with you

When you walk down roads not knowing where they lead
You pick up His Word and on that Word you feed
Then as you walk, His Word you will find
Will keep you in peace in your body, soul and mind

Psalms 23

BE STILL AND KNOW

Don't be washing the dishes
Don't be answering the phone
Don't be running here and there
Finally realizing I gave up and I have gone
Don't be mopping and dusting
Calling yourself talking to me
I am well acquainted with dust
That's what I made you of you see
Don't be carrying out the trash
Or trying to wash and dry the clothes
Just stop, be still and listen to me
If you want to know what Heaven knows
There are a million things you can do
At the same time say you are praying
But, if you are so busy paying attention
How do you keep up with what you are saying?
It's really okay to pray
While you do other things you see
But, when you are quiet and being still
More of your attention is given to me
Talking over noise is very distracting
Busyness means two things are going on
Your attention is anything but undivided
I just want time for us to be alone
Then you can hear much better
We can definitely work some things out
You won't have any trouble hearing me
And I won't have to shout
Love GOD

Luke 10:41-42

SPIRITUAL THERAPY

I have learned the benefit of physical therapy
In helping you recover from injury
I also found God uses spiritual therapy
To try to keep you spiritually injury free
When He comes to talk to me
If I don't have to make a sudden turn
Then I won't inflict pain on myself
From some therapy lesson I did not learn
If I have exercised in the Scripture
And bending of my knees in prayer
Then there will be no sudden impact of injury
When I realize He is there
I won't have to try to hide some things
That I think He don't want to see
For in the haste of trying to appear "spiritual"
I may find myself falling too hard on my knee
If I take benefit frequently from the plan
That my Father has designed for me
Then the strength that it will provide
Will keep me spiritually "injury free"

Numbers 21:9

POWER OF THOUGHTS

There is nothing like being almost asleep
Then a dam breaks letting a flood of thoughts free
The next thing I know every bit of sleep has fled
For a torrent of thoughts are sweeping over me
First come the thoughts of "What did I not do today?"
"Was there something I had great plans for?"
Did I get deterred from what I really wanted to accomplish?
Is that why my thoughts are wanting to war?
Then thoughts of all my failures get thrown in the mire
Wanting to replay every wrong word that I have spoke
Bringing up names that might have some aught against me
Making hopes of sound sleep just fly up in smoke
More thoughts come about what a failure I am
Every bad thing I ever eperienced flashes through my mind
My imagination starts running to find some place to go
Where some kind of resemblence of peace I will find
A new kind of thought starts pushing through the flood
A voice begins to remind me that all these things are in the past
"I have a way for you to stop these tormenting thoughts"
"I have given you a place all these frustrations to cast"
"These kind of thoughts only have the power you allow"
"There is no need to let these thoughts ruin your sleep"
"I have forgiven all your past with my death on the cross"
"Have not I promised your soul I will keep?"
"Don't allow these thoughts to destroy your peace"
"Let go of the past for your future is ahead"
"The only power they can possibly hold over you now
Is just lying there giving them free run in your head"
"Everybody has a past with multiple kinds of regret"
"But, I am your anchor aand will hold you in my power alone"
"If you will remember the price of your redemption is paid
I have given you the power to make sure they are gone"

Jeremiah 29:11

STORMS SHOULD MAKE US STRONGER

If you set out your own ship to sail
The sky is blue and the sun is bright
It makes for a great day to lift anchor
for the world today seems quite alright
Out into the deep you go
Exploring what will come your way
Enjoying all that your eyes can see
Looking forward to another great day
Then the morning comes with no sun
The sky is still as dark as night
Time seems to be standing so still
As the darkness delays the morning light
The day is not starting with joy
We realize today won't be much fun
The darkness is bringing us the news
Today, there will be no sun
The storm is coming on very strong
We will have to ride it out in the boat
It looks like one of those wild ones
Where only God can keep us afloat
The storms of life can really test us
We learn how to sail with each new trial
We can grow and change with each experience
Or close right up and live in denial
We sometimes have to stay in the storm
Till it seems we can hang on no longer
God's hand will stay on us until it is over
He just expects us to come out stronger

Hebrews 11:33-34

THE MOUTH OF FEAR

Fear has a very large mouth
He uses it to beat you down
We have to be careful how loud he gets
For his constant battering brings a constant frown

His mouth is his most valuable tool
For one word can bring on a flood
Of negative thoughts full of hell's torment
Making my brain feel like mud

The louder he talks his trash to me
The muddier my brain becomes
It sounds like a huge battle breaking out
The warriors are beating their drums

Faith comes quietly in to take over
Softly speaking great peace to me
If I stop and acknowledge his voice
Fear can't stand and he has to flee

His mouth has to close and his words cease
Faith in the boldness of God's strength takes charge
Fear may have a very big mouth
But, God's strength and power are extremely large

Matthew 10:28

WHERE IS OUR FOCUS

Problems should not be a distraction
Causing us to avoid what God tells us to do
Our reactions should be cool and calm
For God promises His peace is true
Evil loves it when we despair
To the point we are of no use
God has to teach us over again
Despair is a tool for evil's abuse
If you look at your own circumstance
Your focus narrows to such a point
Your own life seems to unravel
And you're falling apart at every joint
Then a world full of hurting people
Pass you by on every side
You are so engrossed in a pin-point stare
Your desire to help has all but died
There comes a time when you must deal
With your own problems still in your sight
But, God will balance you with His will
Making sure it turns out right
Some of our problems come in a way
They are not what they seem at all
Only distractions that ring the alarm
Making us jump at their beck and call
We must trust God with these distractions
Keep our focus on what we know is true
Before we know it God has performed a miracle
Our problems are diminished and we have done His will, too

Hebrews 12:1-

UNBREAKABLE PROMISES

When you can't see through your eyes
What God is wanting to do
If you fret and fuss about it
It can bring destruction to you
If you spend all your time
Wondering does God really care
It is a major tool evil uses
To get you into despair
God works in His own time
To bring about His desire
Even when you can't see Him "doing"
He expects you to trust He is there
His Word of promise is faithful
He will never leave or forsake
His promises are written eternal
He cannot even the least one break
What He says He will do
But, only in His time and way
When you struggle and start to worry
Refresh to yourself what does His word say
Don't ever lay it aside and avoid it
Take time to read it and pray
When you can't see what God is doing
You'll rest assured He's still in your day

II Cor 1:20

GOD'S TIGHT GRIP

I found myself feeling like
God was letting go His hold on me
Until I realized that I was my own problem
God's way I was failing to see
I was not putting into practice
The lessons I had already learned
I was the blocker of communication between God and me
I had caused my own feelings to turn
God has promised He would never let go
Once I had given up my stubborn will
My emotions were causing me to be angry
Satan, with lies, my mind began to fill
Too many problems coming too fast
Had caused my faith to begin to erode
I found myself had weakened my grip
I had begun traveling my own desperate road
It didn't take long for me to find
I was my own problem in this case
I wasn't listening to God for my own needs
I was not using His great gift of Grace
I sat down before Him in great sorrow
Confessing my anger at what I had let go wrong
I found that His grip was tighter than I could imagine
His arms were around me just where they belong

Psalms 91:11

ANGER ADVANCES NOTHING GOOD
ETERNALLY REWARDING

When things start to happen
Over which you have no control
Anger begins to rise up inside
Methodically tormenting your soul
You can find yourself in such a state
That you can't feel anything but mad
If you could just get to something or someone
You would show them the temper you had
All the thoughts of "it's not fair"
"Don't it just seem that I have had enough?"
"Instead of things getting better for me
It seems they just got more tough"
But, then I realize my greatest problem
Is letting myself react this way
For someone gently reminded me
Why not just go to God and pray?
It's not how the problem is affecting me
That should be the frustration I feel
It should be the other souls needing Christ
That need to repent and be healed
What I need to do right now
Is give up my need for vengeance to find
Let God's peace come back in control
Quieting my heart and soul and mind
Let Him take care of what caused the anger
Remember He can do far more than me
Allowing Him to solve the problem
All involved will His glory and power see

James 1:19-20

ETERNAL BLESSING

In those weak moments
When despair starts to scream
My stomach knots in strange fashion
Evils face starts to beam
God takes me to His Word
or reminds me of a place
Where we had already met
And shared His wonderous grace
He shows me in another time
Where His love sufficient has been
He had so graciously rescued me
Now, my heart forms a grin
When I feel so empty inside
and the world keeps spinning around
I am so thankful for God's ways
That He keeps away my frown
His word brings life into focus
Jesus died for my life to be the best
He made sure that I could live in peace
And look forward to Eternal Rest

John 17:3 I Timothy 6:12

HEARING VOICES?

We all have times in our lives
When we hear voices galore
So many thoughts and suggestions at one time
Very seldom silence, always one more
Some are louder than others
Wanting your attention over the rest
Before you respond to any one of them
You should put them to this test
What is the voice telling you?
Is it something that God would say?
Is it connected with some lesson from Heaven?
Is it going to consume your day?
God says His sheep know His voice
To another one they will not respond
They are so aware of their Master's voice
To another there is no bond
If the voice is loud and boisterous
From it you need to tune out
God's still small voice causes your faith to grow
Loudness causes you to have more doubt
When all the voices start challenging
Remember you can make the right choice
God's power is what causes you to hear Him
You will know which is His voice

I Samuel 3:8-10

RISEN SON

The battle is on, the fighting is fierce
The darts of evil, my soul, do pierce
It is all I can do to stand and not run
I am like Joshua, I see the setting sun
If night comes and no victory in sight
The foe will have advanced as we see dawns light
We can't stand alone through dark midnight hours
The fears are too great for victory to be ours
We must be victorious, together we stand
Uplift one another and hold to God's mighty hand
The battle is raging, whose Captain is greater
We should not let this go on much later
Who will be the winner? Whose leader will stand?
My God has promised victory, I am in His hand
I still see the setting sun, darkness is creeping on
The battle seems hopeless and I want to run
But, through the darkness I see another light
It gives me strength to finish the fight
The battle is turning, the foe is gone
The light that I see, THE RISEN SON

Luke 24:34

HIS HEALING TOUCH

When I feel really bad
Sickness gets me down
It seems that it is too easy
For me to be sad and frown

My body doesn't like me
I get too attached to the bed
My stomach just won't get unqueasy
I am dizzy in my head

When I stand the room starts spinning
I rush to sit back in my chair
I know my countenance isn't pretty
I don't really seems to care

But, I know one thing for certain
Of this I am positive and sure
Every illness in my life
My Jesus has the cure

He cured the problem for my sin
He washed them all away
The physical illness that I feel
He takes care of them His way

I know I will get through it
He has brought me through so much
Whether forgiveness for sin or physical healing
There's nothing like His touch

Isaiah 53:5

OUR ANGEL FACES

When you are in the midst
Of strong adverse weather
God has a wonderful way
To bring His people together
Just to let you know
You are not alone
He has His angels everwhere
Just to keep your faith strong
They bring gentle reminders
He is guiding your steps each day
Don't let your troubles take control
His angels are stationed along the way
When you are alone
Everything seems out of place
I know for sure if you look in the right direction
God will show you an angel's face

Matthew 4:6a-6b

HAVE YOU SEEN JOY LATELY

I was having one of those days wondering
Where in the world had my joy gone
Had it taken vacation and didn't let me know
I decided I had better look and see what was wrong
Worry began to creep upon me
Making me wonder if my Joy I would find
For it seems I had become so frustrated lately
It had really begun to affect my mind
I had been having a real problem with anger
That was leaving me feeling quite depressed
Other problems were piling up drowning my hope
I was giving into pressure that was keeping me stressed
No one else in the world could be feeling like this
Lonliness had really turned my face into a frown
I was in such dire straits that I had not had the time
To see that unhappiness was bringing me down
My joy had just up and waltzed right out the door
I found that it had no desire to hang around
When myself wants to be in power and reign
No wonder my joy could not be found
Then the thought "THE JOY OF THE LORD IS MY STRENGTH"
I asked the Lord to kick all this other stuff out
First the worry, the frustration and the anger
Then depression, hopelessness, self pity and doubt
I then asked the Lord to forgive me
For letting myself try to sit on His throne
Then I saw His joy shining right through me
For it had forced all that hid my joy to be gone

Psalms 30:5

WHY ALL THE WAITING?

Do you ever wonder
Why God seems to take so long
To send an answer to a problem
Or possibly right something so wrong?

We all have to learn some lessons
That change in our life will bring
God is wanting to change our thinking
Or, give us a new song to sing

He wants us to be ready
To seize His change with gratitude
He doesn't like us to be "stuck in the mud"
But willing to change our attitude

Waiting is always for a reason
A problem usually involves more than one
Each one has to be "touched" by the Father
Before there can be a positive outcome

Waiting can often cure two or three things
Depending on how involved emotions are
We have time to ponder on our response
Wanting God to be the victor by far

He wants us to have the mindset
To appreciate The things He has turned
During our time we find ourselves waiting
Look for other lessons there to be learned

Psalms 27:14

GOD GIVEN CHANCES

God gives us chance after chance
With our own eyes to behold
All the things that He has promised
That are more valuable than gold

The sunrise that we see
The first thing on a new morn
The shine of a moon lit night
When the full moon is first born

The color of the musicians He created
That flutter and sing their warbled song
That has to be very right in God's big world
For that kind of beauty can hold no wrong

The flowers that are so beautiful and bold
Waving in the breezes to beckon us to see
We are here to make your world alive with color
Please take time to tiptoe through me

He gives us all things to make our life good
He loves for us to see through His own heart
Letting Him have control and joy of guidance
In the very first place He wants us to start

Chance after chance is given from Father, God
It's our fault if our enjoyment is not complete
He counted it all joy to be able to give it to us
to enjoy His creation is a sacrifice sweet

II Cor 5:17

SAVORING MY SAVIOR

This time of year is so special in many ways
There are lots of changes my eyes were allowed to see
Of all the years with presents under the tree for Christmas
This year with none is the best for me

Things have happened all through the year
That I know has been in God's plan for my life
Things that normally would have been so upsetting
Have not been a source of any kind of strife

I have learned to live my one day I have today
Allowing God to walk me through each phase
Totally engulfed in God's love and mercy
Knowing that He is planning in His ways

There is a surreal feeling flowing all around me
So comforting and powerful that worry goes away
I am filled with such great expectation from it all
That I listen for everything that He has to ssy

Any provision that I may be lacking in the flesh
Is compensated by knowing in His arms I am bound
Feeling such compassion and mercy directly from Heaven
No greater present could ever be found

There is not a tree big enough to handle the package
It would take to hold the love of God that I feel
Sharing the time just enjoying His presence
Sure makes this time of the year so wonderfully real

I Tim 4:10 II Tim 1:12

HARD LIFE LESSONS

Why do life lessons have to be so hard?
Why do some seem to never end?
Why do we have to be so hard-headed?
Why does our will become so hard to bend?

When will we get to where they can cease?
When will we be allowed some not so hard?
When will we enter some graduation phase?
When will we get our free-pass card?

Where can we find the source of these lessons?
Where is the book with some answers of ease?
Where is the place in our life to appear
Where we don't have to stay on our knees?

How is it that we need so many lessons?
How many more before they become less?
How is it that age seems to bring more?
How do the lessons prevent a regress?

What will be the outcome of the lessons?
What will we know instead of guessed?
What will be the answer to all these questions?
What is the result of a half-learned test?

Why does God love us enough to send the lesson?
When will He see that His plan is complete?
Where will we stand when He asks the questions?
How will we feel when we bow at His feet?

What will be the result of our judgment?
What will the answer be when we ask to be allowed in?
What will matter about the lessons when we see His face?
What will stop the tears when we realize our sin?

Galatians 2:20

LET GO AND LIVE

There's nothing in this world worth holding on to
If it's going to cheat us out of God's blessing
We will hold on until we are so attached to it
Not realizing that our life is spent just guessing
Is this all that my life is going to be worth?
Is this really what God wants of me?
Will I ever move on from this one problem?
God, am I really where you want me to be?
God will use anything that comes in our life
To teach us of Him and His great plans
We can't allow circumstances to get us in a rut
For then we will forget our lives are in His hands
We have to learn to let go and move on
When we have learned what God has for us
In any problem in life that we face
It's all a matter of who we trust
Even in the midst of the problem
WE can rejoice as we allow God to teach
Any lesson for us that will cause us to surrender
Knowing we are never out of His reach
Let your problems become a matter of celebration
For God has great blessings in store
When He is finished teaching you in any given one
There is always another with His blessings galore
Change the way you look at what is happening
Your life may be far more happy than you think
It's only when the circumstances rule us
That we can know that life really can stink

Matthew 6:21

THE EROSION OF WORRY

The Lord tells us not to worry about tomorrow
He also tells us why we should obey
If we worry about all that could happen in the future
It takes the strength He gives us for today

If we worry to the extreme about tomorrow
Then feeble will be our attempt for the "now"
God has the knowledge to know all that is coming
Our concern is to trust, His concern is for the how?

Troubles are a bother and a distraction
When we are trying to make trust our devotion
We have to remember as we learn and gain wisdom
That trust, like love, cannot be built on emotion

Faith is the key unlocked by the hearing of God's Word
The same Word that formed the Earth and breathed life into us
He spoke it, it worked! It's up to us to believe it
With the backing of the power in the Word of God
WHY SHOULD IT BE DIFFICULT FOR US TO TRUST?

Psalms 37:3

RESPONDING TO GOD'S VOICE

I am sitting here listening for God's voice
Listening and waiting to make my choice
To honor Him with my heart full of praise
Letting Him know I walk in His ways
The day has been full of pain and confusion
One of evils plans to bring me delusion
But, I have learned when so much is going on
To stay with my Father until I don't need to groan
He has been with me asking me to hear
Him telling me in soft voice that He is near
He has asked me to look up and see
All the beautiful parts of life He is showing to me
My pain doesn't bother me nearly so much
When I realize I am enjoying my Father's touch
Confusion is there only as a decoy
Making me whine and cry at all that does annoy
I will trade my pitiful, whining attitude
For my Father's mercies and all that is good
He will expose me to them as He exposes my need
For my soul to be fed and on His Word feed
There should be no time in my day to entertain doubt
God has shown me so many times His amazing ways out
Of all the things that I can let pull me down
He lifts me up when He makes Satan frown
So, Father speak to me in tone deep and clear
Remove all doubt, worry and fear
I will praise you with heart full of song
Especially when so many things seem to go wrong
As you read these words and realize it is true
Satan will do the same things to you
But, the joy of submission for freedom in your days
Is to respond to our Father with a heart full of praise

John 10:4

Praise Him Forever and Ever

Praises go to God today
For the great things He has done
Praises and worship to my great Father
For I know He is the One
The One with all the power
My every need to meet
It's very appropriate for me to worship Him
To bow myself at His feet
It doesn't seem quite enough
Just to send Him this praise
For He sends all this goodness to me
Not just for one but all of my days
I praise Him for His faithfulness
For He is always a present help
I don't have to worry over anything
For I know He guides my every step
He is a wonderful and compassionate friend
He has promised to quell my every fear
I don't have to be afraid of anything
He has promised to always be near
I praise Him for His compassion
For the promise they will never fail
He has them new and waiting each morning
That's why I am so eager to tell
Of all the things He has done for me
How my life is covered with His touch
I can look to Calvary where He took my sin
Seeing how He loves me so much
Knowing that His love so abounds
that He paid the price for my sin
Keeps me willing to lift my voice
Praising Him time and time again

Hebrews 13:15

WHAT A SON

I am so glad my Heavenly Father
Introduced me to His Son
He assured me in getting to know Him
I would find that He is the One
The One that I can depend on
The One whose love is true
The One that will be with me
No matter what I walk through
He said His faithfulness would amaze me
He would never leave my side
He would be a place of safety
where I can always run and hide
He said He would protect me
Angels would always hover near
He said to remember to always stand strong
I don't have to live in fear
He said things are not always what they seem
That is why it is such a "must"
To let Him have His way in my life
It's all a matter of trust
He reached out His hand to me
Asking me to believe what He said
He burned it right into my heart
As I felt the scar where He had bled
The look in His eyes was so intense
Love was all that I could see
He said all that He ask in return
You simply trust in ME

John 3:16

GOD, DID YOU SAY WAIT?

Waiting is something not easily done
It can be bothersome and not any fun
It is not our nature to just stand and wait
Too much of it causes joy to abate
When God says "do it" we try to obey
For surely we won't have to WAIT but a day
But, when the waiting goes on for years
We are reduced to tearing eyes and massive fears
Faith takes courage and a strong belief
That God's promises in His "time" will bring relief
During the time the waiting takes place
God will send you truck loads of grace
His presence and teaching are valuable tools
If we don't get tired of His "manna" and retreat like fools
Many times waiting will do much to prepare
For the miracle that is coming that time will share
Sometimes the waiting may hang around and haunt
But, what a miracle you will miss if you don't
WAIT!

Psalms 27:13

A Simple Reminder

Sometimes I need a simple reminder
When things are getting to me
That Jesus bore the worst of my pain
When He was nailed to a tree

Sometimes I need a simple reminder
When evil tries to convince me I am lost
Jesus had a crown of thorns on His head
As for my sin, He paid the cost

Sometimes I need a simple reminder
When there are bills that I can't pay
Jesus cares for the birds and the flowers
But, for me in a far better way

Sometimes I need a simple reminder
When problems come with no answers in sight
Jesus wants me to give Him all my trust
He is the one to make all things right

Sometimes I need a simple reminder
When harsh persecution I have to face
That's when God speaks so strong and sweet
"Child, sufficient is all my grace"

The next time I need a simple reminder
When things are piling up on me
I hope that I can simply say "Thank You, God"
"Forever grateful to You I will be"

Isaiah 1:18

WHO ARE YOU BRINGING GLORY TO

Worry is glorifying evil
Letting him bring you to his level
It's like you are standing and applauding
What you have heard from the devil
He doesn't have a book of answers
Like God has given you to find
He just gets into your thoughts
Starts messing with your mind
How is it that we believe him
We listen more to what he has said
When God has given us His Holy Word
That we should have sat down and read
God's power is inside those pages
It's up to us a weapon to form
It will counteract any thing the devil uses
To cause our day to start to storm
God will drive away the worry
If we applaud and submit our will
He delights in speaking up for us
Using words like "PEACE BE STILL"

Romans 12:2

Joy Sticks Like Glue

There ain't nothing gonna stand in the way
Of God's great joy I am feeling today
There's not a reason for me to frown
Ain't nothing gonna bring my joy down

God gave me joy when evil tried to make me sad
My mind was worried about things going bad
But, the joy of the Lord is stronger than strong
He keeps me happy when all else goes wrong

I say Joy is in my heart today
God's kind of joy that won't go away
The kind that keeps me going the extra mile
The kind that covers all saddness with a smile

Joy that makes a song for my heart to sing
Joy that bans worry over what tomorrow will bring
Joy in knowing I can depend on God's Word
Joy that gives me peace when His voice I have heard

I tell you again nothing can take my joy
Nothing in this world is strong enough to annoy
To the extent that God's voice I can't hear
Joy will keep me standing without any fear

John 15:11

CIRCUMSTANCE SHOULD CAUSE THANKFULNESS

You can be thankful in every circumstance
For everything has a lesson for you
God wants to know in all that happens
What is the first known thing you do
Is it fear that comes to overwhelm
To try to stomp and crush you down?
Or, is it the warmth of God's Holy presence
That replaces with a smile that depressing frown?
God wants to know in the worst of times
That you don't turn on Him with blame
But, you choose to stand in victory
Trusting Him Wholly in Jesus Name
Give Him praise and worship He is due
He truly gives us peace and strength to stand
All it takes to get what we need from Him
is just a show of Praise by one raised hand

Psalms 95:2

I Can't Stand Alone

I am so thankful that God has let me see
That I must continually build on relationship between Him and me
The more we build the more I can stand
Knowing that He is in control and I am led by His hand
When I take over and try to go my way
It doesn't take long to see what makes a bad day
I can't even begin to see what His eyes can see
That is why He must be the leader, leading me
He knows how to turn away from every evil foe
He always knows the right way to go
I must not waste time struggling against Him
He is the light that is shining when all else is dim
I know that He is a master builder with plans
That will get me where He wants, led by His hands
So, I will ask Him daily to teach me to build
My way to Him in everything, yield
Yes, I am thankful that He builds so well
My thankfulness to Him, I so willingly will tell

I Cor 3:10-11

VALUE OF A GOOD FRIEND

God has taught me the value
Of having a really good friend
Especially going through the rough times
When heart and soul are on the mend

There is nothing like having a friend
That has gone through what you are now in
They become your personal cheering squad
Cheering you on time and again

They know just when to call you
Or even drop by to give you a cheer
You can get a card in the mail box
With words that cancel your fear

The ability to understand where you are
Is a gift of understanding God has sent
They know how to encourage where you are going
And praise you for escaping the place you just went

The truth of how to survive anything
A good friend can present to you
For when you are in the survival mode
You don't always know what to do

But, a friend that has conquered the trial
And on the mountain top now does stand
Is the one you want to stand by you
And hold out that encouraging hand

Proverbs 17:17

THE MORNING SCHEDULE

I have become so aware of time consuming chores on my list
Required to get ready for work; keeping on schedule with nothing missed
I first get up and take my trip to relieve the pressure from the night
Out goes the dog for its turn, watching and making sure she is alright
The feeding and getting her settled, eat my food and swallow some pills
Check my sugar and my blood pressure making sure I have no ills
Then, deciding what to wear and plug in the curling iron to get hot
Get my bath and groom myself making sure nothing is forgot
On goes the lotion, makeup and such, body sprays and perfumes for smell
Trying to make sure I look good at least as far as I can tell
Then the hair, what a trial; sometimes it does fall in place
But thank God the iron is hot; I am trying to rush and not burn my face
Get the jewelry to match the shirt, grab the pants and match the shoes
One little something out of place will dare someone to share the news
Feed the dogs in the pen not forgetting the fish in the pond
Lay out something for supper, Heaven help me! It's run, run, run
Check my email and checking account just making sure no bad news
Need my day to be cheerful and not entertaining any blues
In the car and on my way, cell phone and purse in plain view
Then I wonder what I had forgot and God says:
"WHERE IS MY TIME WITH YOU?"

II Cor 13:4

AROUND THE MOUNTAIN AGAIN?

When the same old problem keeps coming around
What lesson is it that I have not learned?
What is going on inside me
That to God, that part I have not turned?
Is it me that still needs the lesson?
It does not cause the problem that once it did
Is there some emotion still inside me
That the results of it I want to keep hid?
There is a temporary anger that appears
When I feel like I am back at the start
It makes me feel like there will not be
Another resson for the beating of my heart
But in a moment it is gone away
For my memory is reminded to stay strong
It's not a crime to have the emotion
I just can't let my reaction be wrong
I think the anger that appears
Is a far stronger force than I will admit
It tries to turn into a quiet hatred
And it would surely succeed
If God didn't remind me to quit
Quit looking at the return performance
That would love to destroy me still
Keep my focus on what God wants of me
Keeping me in His perfect will

Matthew 17:20

GOD AND ME

God and I are doing just fine
He has so changed this life of mine
He took something that would usually annoy
Using it to fill me with such joy
Everyday is a new challenge to me
Wanting to share Jesus with everyone I see
Trying to cheer someone that is sad
Showing life with God is anything but bad
He has taught me to trust and believe
That's what it takes, from Him to receive
God has told us He will not lie
Therefore, there is no reason to cry
His mercy is abundant in whatever we face
Covered with goodness and flooded with grace
He sends unspeakable joy to overcome fear
The joy is knowing He is always near
His presence is a gift to make us aware
Where we are continually blessed with all He will share
There is enough to conquer all evil can send
For God, Himself, has promised to defend
All His children that love Him so much
He can handle it with His powerful touch
I am so glad that God and I are fine
For I am fully blessed by ONE so divine

John 17:9-10

THERE COMES A TIME

When it comes time that it's declared
You must put into action
All the things God has taught you
To bring about a right reaction
It's easy to look at the words on paper
Wondering if it's true what you've been told
The time is now to believe knowing you will receive
If you ever intend to be God's witness, bold
The blessings obedience will bring are real
God said to do it and the words are plain
Obedience should always be practiced NOW
You must follow Him, His peace to gain
It's true He spoke His words in power
You speak it out just like He said
Now, it's your turn, now is your hour
Like you have heard and from the paper read
Believe every word that you know He spoke
Whatever the situation and emotion involved
Remember how your spirit inside He awoke
He has the way to overcome, every problem be resolved
God doesn't ever waste His time
How you react determines what will abate
He is never more ready to act
Than when your pain is so great
There always comes a NOW time
God will put into use every lesson
And He truly has the power needed
To stop every known aggression
God's lessons have the purpose of showing you
You have to obey and stand in the belief
That your obedience in the NOW time
Will bring His blessed relief

I Cor 10:13

WHAT OCCUPYS YOUR HEART?

Have you ever had a feeling in your heart
There was something seriously awry?
It seems there's a big empty spot
You could fill with tears if you began to cry

Sometimes the tears can be useful
They can wash away impurities of the heart
those places we feel inside of us
Are "sore spots" with which we don't want to part

It can be some sort of resentment
It can be self-pity or "woe is me"
It can be a list of "what has been done"
things that keep our heart from being free

These kind of thing won't let the heart feel good
They will grow and push out the best
The more they occupy that place inside of us
We will not find God's perfect peace and rest

If we want to have peace with God
Avoid those days we just want to cry
We must run to God with every hurt
Make sure we don't let unneeded things stay and occupy

Isaiah 26:13

TIME FOR JESUS

When you are feeling the weight of the load
You feel like you are at the end of the road
It is time to call for Jesus

When your feelings are all strung out
Yourself and your abilities you begin to doubt
It's great time to call for Jesus

Just like David keeping his sheep from the bear
He was alone and wondering did anyone care
But, he knew to call for Jesus

For action God was getting Him ready
His aim had to be sure and steady
He had him practicing hour after hour

What he did, didn't seem like much
But, when God added His great touch
That rock resounded God's great power

You don't ever have to feel alone
But, when you are tired and your strength is gone
Jesus will do what He has promised to do

He said He would stay till the end
He will give you strength and your feelings mend
Determination will suddenly come anew

When you know you need His help
He will give what you need for one more step
His Father did the same for His Son

Don't ever think that you have to fail
Go to God and your worries tell
He will give you strength, the race to run

Jeremiah 16:19

WHAT YOU GONNA DO?

God puts people in your path everyday
Some may need to talk, some may need to pray
What you gonna do?

Some may have a heavy load to bear
Some may just need someone to care
What you gonna do?

Some may need a friend really bad
Some may need to deal with being so sad
What you gonna do?

Some may need your big gracious smile
Some may need one to go the second mile
What you gonna do?

God puts these people there for a reason
You will or you will not make a decision
What you gonna do?

When God ask, "Do you remember when
I sent this person to you once and some again?"
What you gonna do?

I John 2:17

WRONG FOCUS MAKES ME A WHINER

It seems fairly easy to say
Not my will, Father but Thine
But when things begin to happen
I become a champion of WHINE
Why does it have to be so much?
Why does this load weigh me down?
Father, I know You want me to smile
But, all I can do is frown
I can handle one or two things
But, the count is heavy now
I know that I should trust You more
But, I think I have forgotten how
What is that you are saying, Lord?
I have to change my attitude
I have to quit focusing on how tough it is
How people are so uncaring and rude
You told me that is how it is
How I must go in Jesus' Name
I can't keep looking at all the problems
For then I will do nothing but blame
I have to look in Your eyes
I have to believe what YOU have said
I must focus on what I know to be true
Quit letting the problems fill my head
I know that when You were tired, Jesus
You asked if possible that the cup could pass
But, our Father knew it had to be

He gave you strength to last
I know I don't have to face the things
That You had to go through
But, I don't want to be a whiner either
I want to be as victorious as You
So, Father, help me with the questions
Let me only ask the important one
When I have finished with what you have ask
I want to know Your will is done

Phil 4:13

PRAYING FOR A FRIEND

Father, if I could have your attention for a moment
I want to tell you about my friend
She is having problem on top of problem
A great supply that seems without end
It seems she is growing weary, Father
She is waning and losing her strength
She won't be able to get much farther, Lord
If they continue too much longer in length
Please help her to understand Your strength
You will give it to her every day
You will take the load for her and bear it
If she will listen to what you say
It gets so tough as the burden grows
Even knowing that You are near
But, help her to not get so busy in the bearing
That your encouragement she can't hear
Show her how to "lay it down"
To put the burden at Your feet
Let her relish the promise that You have made
That Your peace will abide so sweet
Give her the kind that passes understanding
The kind that will level things out
The kind that will replace her fear with strength
The kind that will remove her doubt
Let her learn to trust you completely
Let her heart, Your hope retain
Let her, Your mercy and compassions see
Give her great joy and happiness without end
Thank You for hearing me, Father
I am one that has already been made free
Let her know that she can depend on YOU
Just like you have shown it to me Amen

Phil 4:6

CHANGE OF POSITION?

In any situation you are facing
When the slightest of change against you comes
the enemy begins to whoop and holler
Dragging out the "victory drums"
He begins to make a very large to-do
Just like he has won it all
You know he wants to "CUT YOU DOWN"
But, you are standing a little too tall
The enemy can forget it's not me fighting
My God is standing in my place
He is still totally on guard
I am still hidden in His grace
God has the power to reposition
To place me anywhere He does please
The enemy can't tell just where I am
But, it's mostly on my knees
I am not trying to hide from him
I know my God will handle that battle for me
I am bowing to the one that will win
He always has a position of victory

I John 5:4

REAL SURVIVAL

What does it mean to survive?
Knowing that disaster has not won
To overcome adversity with joy of being alive
You are still in the race, willing to run
Your running shoes are all laced up
You are heading for the victory line
Surviving is knowing you will make it
God will make it all end just fine
As long as you keep running
Living water won't let you dehydrate
God will give His strength continually
There is no worry the Source will abate
I am created to be a survivor
God's plan for me will prevail
The way He prepares for me to survive
I will be more than willing to tell
I have all faith and trust in my God
His love for me I will share and tell
Then, when the story of survival is told
I will know it has been told well

II Timothy 4:7

THANK YOU GOD

God has sent so many blessings my way today
There is not too much left to say
Except, Thank You God

His hand is appearing from everywhere
Placing in my hands what He is so willing to share
That is so like my Jesus

I should shut down any thought to complain
Replace those thoughts with Praise to my Father's Name
I know He is waiting

I won't delay and make Him wait
I'll praise Him now with words for my Father, so great
I know He will hear me

The words will come straight from my heart
A chain reaction I know it will start
Causing someone else to praise Him, too

That's what God's goodness is all about
He gives so much to us we all should shout
Thank You, God

Psalms 100:4

HIDDEN THINGS

Have you ever felt as though
God had hidden something from you
Because you got up with something on your mind
Counting your minutes, but He wanted a few
He loves to have the early time
When your mind is fresh and new
For He knows that you will get busy
You will move Him on your "list of to do"
He wants to hear your first words
Even if He heard the last one before sleep
It makes His heart fill with gladness
After all, He tends closely to His sheep
He so watches over us
He knows that precious is the time
He has to show He is our source of comfort
In the early morning, before the sun does shine
When He sees that we are busied
With our list of to do
It's going to be nearly impossible
To have that closeness with you
He just simply hides some things
A lesson to us to teach
He knows that we know to visit with Him
So, He just puts some things out of reach
In all our frustration and worry
For all these things to find
He allows the Holy Spirit to come
To make impressions on our mind
"I am here and it is morning
You have already been busy the best part"
"I have hidden some things from you
So, you can hide some in your heart"

Matthew 10:26

Can You Imagine

Have you ever sat and wondered
Trying to imagine how Jesus must have felt
When He said to the world, "I love You!"
Not a heart did He see melt

Have you tried to imagine
How His tears so heavily did flow
When the nails pierced into His hands
No sympathy did anyone show

Have you closed your eyes to imagine
How the thorns were pushed into His brow
Being mocked and slapped and spit in His face
Wondering why someone didn't rescue Him now

Can you imagine Him suffering for us
When He sees the world do the same thing again
But, He says if we follow in His footsteps
That we will have to be partakers of His pain

Imagine if you will through the inflicted pain
God's grace and mercy come to you in a flood
Our pain should not be anything nearly as bad as His
For He is the one that for us shed His blood

When we are mistreated and scorned by evil
We get absorbed in feelings and almost give in
Remember that we have a promise from our Savior
He has been there, So just try to imagine

I Timothy 6:11-15

BIG THINGS, LITTLE THINGS

We should be very careful
About letting little things deal us any abuse
We can get so bound up in small things
That it's very hard to get loose

They seem to have a tormenting ability
That big things can't stand up to
The Bible says it's the little things
That have the ability to make life miserable for you

We seem to be able to cope with big things
We can take the time an answer to find
But, it's the little things that don't seem to end
That can bring such torture to our mind

God doesn't matter if a problem is big or small
He can handle one as well as the other
It's our thinking that makes one seem impossible
While we can totally cope with another

When we are in such torment over any one
It doesn't matter to God if big or small
If we bring it and let Him know we trust Him
He will show us how He can handle it all

Song of Solomon 2:15

WHO HAS PROBLEMS

Who out there is any different from me?
when it comes to problems there are none free
We all have enough, plenty to share
But, ours is worse, we often declare
We look at those we think problem free
Wondering, "Why can't life be that good to me?"
We can't see inside at all that is going on
We can't bear how often they moan and groan
The front is put up, no one can see
I think their lifestyle is so appealing to me
I keep looking for all those having fun
Wondering if my life will ever be like that one
I came to realize their fun is all fake
For someone in that group is ready to break
On I go still looking for a perfect pair
Smiles on their face and obviously not a care
I am afraid when found my envy will grow
But, I am learning and this one thing I know
Envy is wasted looking for something not real
Perfection has vanished and here is the deal
We all have our problems, ours can't be beat
Work with what you have or live in defeat
If you go trying to see what else you can get
You will find we are all just alike, I BET!

i Thess 4:13

A Fax Lesson

I was waiting for a fax to come
IT was very important to me
I was only expecting one page
But, got worried after page number three
The one page I was looking for
Was to take care of a great need
But, it still wasn't coming through
After nine pages already did feed
As I came down to the very last page
My document still had not come through
Despair began to try to talk
This is not going to work for you
But, then as the top of the page did appear
I saw that it was the one
Peace took over and my despair subsided
At last the fax was done
Isn't this just like God sometimes
When we are expecting answer to prayer
The days or hours will pass with expectation
But, the answer doesn't seem to be there
We forget that God works on His timetable
He knows exactly when to appear
He wants to teach us of His peace
Not to give in to the torment of fear
We all wait for different things
Depending on what phase of life we are in
We should be able to wait on Him
Jesus waited for death to forgive our sin

Psalms 17:14

WE WILL OR WE WON'T

God's Word is very definite and sure
He says we're His child like a son
He says He will give us good things
He just wants acknowledgement that He is the ONE
The One we are willing to serve
The One we depend on for defense
The One we know will keep us standing
When chaos in the world makes no sense
The One that will give us Daily Bread
The One that is Living Water to drink
The One that is able in every circumstance
To do exceeding above all our small minds think
The One that was dead and is alive
The One arisen and intercedes for us
The One who wants us to love Him so
That only in Him will we trust
The One we will claim as Father
What He says we will rise up and do
The One that we will look for to return
For He has promised to return for us, too
God says you can come to Him
In everything, whether in need or want
You have to trust Him for the answer
For either you believe Him, or you don't

John 1:12-13

WHO SAID?

When you know God has called you
For a special purpose from Him
I guess it's just natural to be criticized
From those who realize it's not them
God will choose whomever He needs
For any specific mission He plans
That person need not fear the outcome
For they are truly held in God's hands
It doesn't keep evil from attacking
He knows his purpose is to defeat
But, knowing God is the greater of the two
Makes following God so sweet
Worry is not a word in God's mouth
Fear is something that He tells us to let go
His is the perfect love that lets us stand
His power is what He will let show
He will accomplish what He needs
In a heart that is willing to obey
It doesn't matter how the world views the job
We just have to know God leads the way
He will open the doors for us
All He asks is our best to try
Jesus will never leave us to walk alone
Like the world walked away and left Him to die

John 18:27

SOUND OF CHARIOT WHEELS

God convinced Pharoah to let His people go
Through miracles of His power He did show
The people loaded up and went their way
Not dreaming Pharoah would pursue them another day
They are heading for the Red Sea new life to find
When they suddenly realize Pharoah is coming behind
Talking about trapped with no where to go
Water up ahead and Pharoah's army about to show
Ever feel like this when you thought victory had come
Then the very next day you hear a familiar war drum
That new victory seems now a temporary win
The enemy has struck with a vengeance again
The chariots are coming with a great cloud of dust
Fear is overwhelming hiding your trust
But, God doesn't live by the way He feels
He is not rattled with the sound of chariot wheels
If He says "stand still" then stand still you must
His power is ready to restore your trust
Whatever is ahead is where God will be
He doesn't look behind like you and me
The Red Sea parted and all Israel did cross
The enemy went in and they suffered the loss
When your trust is in God you must look ahead
His point of victory is in what you tend to dread
His mighty power will erase fear of the unknown
For God will leave peace where He has gone
We can get a new attitude from this story I tell
Your mind can defeat you by where you let it dwell
The sound of chariot wheels don't always mean defeat
God has a plan to bring victory, sweet
He really don't panic at the sound of chariot wheels
With a bold spoken word, your victory He seals

Exodus 14:25

WHAT DID I DO WITH IT?

People can really do some crazy things
Trying to find themselves these days
First one thing and then another
Whatever is the latest craze
Some have to do things the hard way
Of this there is no doubt
They must first find a way in
Then they have to find a way out
It can put you on a "rollercoaster"
Emotions up and down all day
But, you will find they will not listen
No matter what you say
God says we can give this to Him
We don't have to struggle at all
He will take the burden and "fix it"
If we will just take time to call
We have the wonderful privilege
Of putting this all into God's hands
Surrendering it freely and letting go
Is all that He demands
The surrender is hard to do
If you are too emotionally involved
But, you have to let them learn the lesson
If you want the situation resolved
It just seems no matter how much I pray
I still find myself getting mad
Over things I had "given to God"
or at least, I thought I had

James 3:13

SCARS FOREVER

We all have some scars
For some reason or another
Some are so minute they can hardly be seen
Some so large they are a bother

We all have a story to tell
As to how the scars came about
The larger the scar the worse the story
The story loves to get told no doubt

Few scars can make a difference
For the whole world in an eternal way
For most of the scars we walk around with
Were acquired in just a normal day

One man, Jesus, was totally different
He has scars with a real story to tell
The scars that He has to show to the world
Backs up the story of salvation from hell

Just imagine yourself in His wonderful presence
Wanting to see what the story is all about
He looks in your eyes with the greatest of love
While extending His hands right out

Matthew 27:29

A PRAYER

Father, quiet my spirit today
Guard my mouth and the words I say
Calm my fear and remove my doubt
Things in me not needed, take them out
I feel like I'm trying to take control
That's the reason for torment in my soul
You are the force that keeps my life straight
Help me to slow down and quietly wait
For Your direction to where I should go
Your peace and presence I surely will know
I have friends needing your help today
Send it to them in Your Name I pray
Help us to surrender to Your divine will
Taking the time in Your presence to be still

Matthew 6:9-13

REFLECTIONS

As I look in the mirrow this morning
It's supposed to be God's image I see
But, do I worry more about His glory
Or, what I appear to be?
Am I going out to impress the world
With ever hair in place
Or, is it God I want the world to see
A representative of His Glory and Grace
I need to remember as I am looking
Without God I cannot change a thing
So, I need to focus entirely on Him
Let my actions, all glory to Him bring
What makes my life of any value
As my reflection in the mirror I see
Is to be so aware I am the image of God
The world must see Him and never me

John 14:9

GOD IS FOREVER

It wss a week ago this morning
God let me see the cross across the road
Where it was a reminder from HIm
That I could leave my heavy load

All the worry and all the care
That for some time had piled on me
Plus things from just a short time earlier
That had brought a crisis to see

Well, I was looking again about the same time
To see if it would come with this mornings sun
It was a little earlier than the time last week
But, to the window I did run

There it was as bright as day
As beautiful as the one before
I took it's picture just like the other
It enraptured my heart all the more

I stood in awe just feeling so blessed
This is my "special" gift from Heaven today
In my heart I knew I was not alone at all
I heard the whisper of my Father say

"This is the reminder that I will take care of you
You have my promises I will leave you never
If this sight never appears here again
Remember, My promises are forever!"

John 14:23

FEED FEARS FAITH

When you are sitting in doubt
Wondering how you will get out
A little Bible truth may work for you

When you are beginning to mourn
Your faith is being torn
You need to put a little faith to work, it's true

When the voice you are hearing loud
Is the evil one so quick and proud
You need to re-adjust your earphones

When the beat of your heart increases
Causing you to emotionally fall to pieces
Things are really getting into the danger zones

It is time for a dose of God's peace
He promised compassions that never cease
It always comes in the worst of circumstance

You can't live in faith and listen to doubt
You can't be double minded and get out
You have to learn the Father's way to advance

You must believe exactly what He means
He specializes in those "it just seems"
You keep right on doing what He said

Those doubts and fears will have to fade
For the Father says the way is made
When Faith to your fears has been fed

I John 4:18

GOD TAKES THE HEAVY LOADS

Today is trying to be a "heavy" day
It's really trying to dump its trash on me
It's closing in circling around each side
Something doesn't want my spirit free

I will not accept this thing trying to happen
God said the load was not heavy or hard to bear
I want to feel free and full of life
I will put all this day in His care

If evil can make you feel crushed
Your strength will be of no use to you
God wants you to let Him carry the load
Heaviness in your day is over and through

Watch out for those things that try to attach
They will come unnoticed and stick like glue
With God as your watchman and security guard
The heaviness will never even get to you

Psalms 55:22

The Wonderful Strength of God

My life is not about how strong I am
But, how strong I will allow God to be
When I can't do a thing for myself
He said His strength I can see!

God said He will lift me up to the mountain!
He said in the valley He will make me a door!
I can walk through the fire and not be burned!
His strength can do so very much more!

He said the waters might sweep over me!
His strength will not let me drown!
He said that in every thing that I face
His Spirit will wipe away any frown!

His strength comes to me like love!
For love has a power all its own!
God knows that without love in our lives
Any ability that we had will find itself gone!

God's strength has power above all other!
He can accomplish what no other can do!
When I find myself at my weakest time
His strength comes rushing through

He has not given me a Spirit of fear
But, His power, His love and a sound mind!
When there is not strength enough in me
I know the place there is plenty to find

II Cor 12:9

GOOD VS EVIL

Good and evil met on the battlefield
Ready to "fight to the end" which will yield?
Both were armed to the hilt, armor in place
Evil stood glaring, threatening to spit in Good's face

The arrogance of evil declared he had won
Calling himself winner, the battle over before begun
Throwing defiance at Good, just turn yourself and run
Evil is too strong, Good is already outdone

Good stood quietly listening to evil roar
Evil never silent, declaring more and more
You can't stop me; my power is too great
Good, you might as well quit, it's already too late

Good looked at evil and did quietly declare
You will never win; I have a message to share
You only see evil, you think you are so grand
But, Good is more able than you ever to stand

Good will be around when all evil is done
For all good is eternal representing God's Son
Evil wilted, realizing he had suffered a loss
For there where he stood appeared the shadow of Christ's Cross

Romans 12:21

GOD IS ALL I NEED

I don't need another thing
As long as I know God loves me
He shouts His comfort in my direction
I feel it even if I don't see

He covers me with His presence
He fills me with joy divine
I am so content and full of peace
What more do I need in this life of mine?

It's like walking in the garden
In the evening cool of the day
Calling out my name wanting to visit
Talk about doing things His way

I have found that when I listen
Truly follow His plan for me
Not another thing do I need
His love opens the path I see

Phil 4:19

GOD'S GRACE COVERS ME

God's presence overwhelms and uplifts
When the world wants to dump on me
I am not a garbage dump
For evil and what the world wants to see

God will not let me crumble
His strength is anything but frail
When I know I can't help myself
God sends assurance that He will not fail

I know I can stand in Him
He has His ways, His time and place
To see that evil is notified
His child is covered by His grace

James 4:6

GOD'S PLAN FOR DOUBT

When I am plagued with thoughts of doubt
Jesus has His ways to bring me out
He begins by speaking peace to my soul

When pain tries its best to conquer me
Jesus reminds me in Him I am free
All those stripes for healing will keep me whole

When fear tries to turn into gloom
It fills all the space in the room
Jesus feeds His words into my heart like a flood

He reminds me He has conquered fear
He tells me He is always near
All I need to do is live in the power of His blood

God's presence comes into my space
Reminding me of His mercies and grace
They all are sent to me new every day

If I remember to believe what He has said
There's not a reason for me to dread
He is the Truth, the Light and the Way

Oh, yes He will bring me out
Of any space filled with doubt
All my worries and my fears will be still

His power is great and powerful enough
To walk me straight when times are tough
I will surrender every part of me to His will

Romans 14:23

A Cancelled Pity Party

A pity party is in the making
Because I didn't get my way
Something I thought should have happened
Didn't take place in my day
Self-pity got out the tables and napkins
He went back for all the chairs
Up went all the arranged seating flags
With the message "no one cares"
Thoughts of "I deserve better than this"
Took the place of "doing things well"
All of this rushed out in a flood
Until I realized it had come from Hell
None of these thoughts make God happy
My thoughts this morning were Him to please
I have got to make my mind shut up
Let God's Word bring me back to peace
This pity party will become a celebration
For God is the Champion of victory
I just remembered He's in charge of today
His will is all I care to see
I will not react to this self-pity
I will not sit at evils table and dine
God will give me "sufficient" for me
My relationship with Him will grow just fine
I will trust in His mercies new today
I will continue to smile not frown
For this party to become a celebration
God can take the pitiful decorations down

John 20:29

GOD GIVES REAL JOY

You can't walk in joy
Until you have walked in unjoyful places
Joy won't be appreciated
until you share some joyless spaces
Joy becomes important
When you walk where there is none
You will invite Joy in your life
When you meet Jesus, God's Son
The world can't give you Joy
It only gives you seasonal pleasure
Joy the world can't take away
Comes from God's special treasure
Fun is what the devil offers
But, it will end after a while
Joy is given for all eternity
It never takes away your smile
God will do it, give you His joy
In every place with Him you will find
Love, Joy and Peace beyond understanding
God only gives His people the everlasting kind

Psalms 16:11

An Example For God

It is so great to hear from my God
And obey what He says to me
I am His tool to light the way
For another child of His to see
I know that He will not fail me
When I listen to Him and obey
I know that's the same thing He does for them
When they need encouragement in a day
I never know when He will come and ask
Or where it is He will say to go
Fear does not have to be my first concern
For He is the maker of my way I know
Just to watch Him blessing one of His own
Or minister to one who needs His touch
Knowing He loved me enough to use me here
Increases my faith again so much
I always want to listen and obey
When He speaks and invites me to come
Whether in a crowd or just one alone
Father help me to be an uplifter to some
I want to be an example of Joy
Encouraging the lost to seek His way
An example of the One who gave Himself to the world
Holding His light to show them the way

Matthew 5:16

REMINDERS FROM GOD

Today is one of those days God has to remind me
All that He has to go through to make me hear
When evil screams at me with all the volume he has
And God is whispering quietly in my ear
He's reminding me not to react at all
To what I think is taking place
To draw my strength from Him alone
He will cause me to stand in His grace
God is so very faithful and true to His Word
What He says you can fully trust
The world screams loud to make you doubt
Listening for Him to speak is a must
Father, please help me to free my ears
From all the unpleasant thoughts in the air
The world has only one thought in mind
That is to destroy me with a heavy load of care
I know that I can come to You
Cast all my care and rest in your peace
That's how to control all those crazy thoughts
Cause all my imagined problems to cease
Just by looking at circumstance all around the world
Everyday I am reminded of how cruel the world can be
When it seems that good exists no more
I am more reminded of God's faithfulness to me

Lamentations 3:22-23

WHAT ABOUT YOUR HANDS

People want to acknowledge God
But, hold on to the world at the same time
It's a combination that will not work
For God declares, "I want you for Mine"
God doesn't want a half-hearted submission
He wants our hearts given to Him
He gives us power to overcome
When the world pulls us with some whim
Trying to live both ways
Will stretch you to a breaking point
You will have to yield to one or the other
Remember the world will rip your every joint
You can't have one hand in the evil
The other hand trying to be good
Only God can give you real balance
Keeping life peaceful as He promised He would
Trying to serve God and holding on to the world
Will bring you nothing but loss
For in everything Christ is our example
Both His hands were nailed to the cross

Hebrews 12:2

GOD IS STILL IN CONTROL

It is just breathtaking to watch the hand of God
He wants us to know He is still in control
He knows how to get our attention
To let us know He is the guardian of our soul

We should never wonder what kind of Father He is
For He is the ultimate example of love
Perfection is something we dream about here
Only to experience when we are with Him above

We waste our time trying to "figure" Him out
His thoughts are too high above our own
Who can "figure" why Almighty God
For people like us, would send us His Son

I am so thankful that Jesus was willing
To obey His Father even though it meant death
I have no doubt as He hung on the cross
He felt the wind of His Father's breath

God's hand is still on this world
Even though we fight against His ultimate plan
We should never wonder what kind of Father He is
He still has us right in the palm of His hand

Psalms 31:15

THE JOY OF THE LORD

I have read in God's Word
The joy of the Lord is our strength
I have pondered it over and over
And thought of it in great length
It is a joy to be a Christian
To know you are free from sin
Not having to worry about your salvation
Or if Heaven will let you in
It's a joy to share with others
The reason for the joy you feel
Letting them know that God gives the kind
That no enemy can steal
Joy gives you God's great strength
As you travel down life's road
You don't have to stay worn out
From dragging around a heavy load
He takes care of every burden
that frees you up from despair
Letting His joy shine through in you
Letting you rest in His total care
Then you don't have to deal with exhaustion
It's a joy to let everyone around you know
That you have the peace that only God can give
With great joy that can't help but show

John 15:11

THE REAL SHELTER

When the storms come
We want to run and hide
If we belong to God, our Father
He will let us know where "to abide"
Sometimes the abiding is tough
Depending on the severity of the storm
Because we tend to look for a "real place"
Where we will suffer the least amount of harm
Storms can be studied to learn
How to prepare for the least amount of loss
But, we don't stop to really consider
The "safety" of the Cross
The eternal shelter it provides
Is where the ultimate safety lies
There is no safer place to hide
When the soul for protection cries
We naturally tend to fear a storm
Being afraid of the unknown magnifies fear
Fear can do more damage than the storms
Its strength is so loud that is all we hear
When we are all worn out with the struggle
Feel like we will lose our mind
God still is trying to make us realize
He is he real place, shelter to find

Psalms 46:1

OF ALL THINGS TO WONDER

Just a wondering tonight
As the rain falls outside
What is the purpose of life?
How do we run to God and hide?

The rain falls to the ground
Bringing hope anew to all it drenches
How does it compare to the water of life?
The power to change the thirst it quenches

New growth comes after the rain
Hydrading the earth with exciting new hope
Making us wonder why we coined the phrase
Tie in a knot and hand on to the rope

We don't have to hang on to rope
God is far stronger and safer than thread
We can know He will hold on to us tightly
He strengthened His grip when on the cross He bled

The purpose of life is to rely on God
Give Him the place in us that He can dwell
In our hearts and we will carry the news
He is alive, come let us tell

As it rains ourside tonight
God reigns inside with me
We don't have to sit and ponder silly things
For hiding in Him, lets us be free

Romans 5:17

DAILY COMMUNICATION WITH GOD

Without my daily communication with God
My strength begins to wane
I get so weak and can't help myself
I begin to act like someone insane
Just one day without His Word
Doesn't cause harm that I can see
But, the second day without my prayer
Begin to pull the strength from me
If I dare to go another day
without time to bend my knees
Satan finds new ways to torment
Wanting to control my day as he does please
Greater is my God that lives within
Than the one that the world will see
God's Word is my power and strength
Through it God wins my victory
I must not let any days pass
Without filling my mind with His Word
Else when the tempter comes to torment me
Words leaving my mouth may not need to be heard
Day by day, each minute and hour
God's Word in my heart is what I must heed
For if I commune this closely with Him
He alone will tend my every need

Acts 17:11

THE USELESS JUNK DRAWER

I made another trip to the "drawer"
I found another item there is no use for
It just seems to remind me of another issue
That should be discarded like a used tissue

Things that are buried in the drawer so deep
There is no earthly reason the thing to keep
Still they hide knowing they will one day appear
Feeling safe in the drawer because of my fear

It's my fault these things can hide
In that drawer, just like my heart inside
When you have forgotten they were ever there
They suddenly appear like dust in the air

What an effect it can have coming out
You know immediately it's a problem, no doubt
it should have been dumped a long time ago
You are a much better person for letting it go

Don't leave it there to bring pain from the past
Swap it now for God's peace that will last
You will know you have won the war
When you empty and discard the junk in the drawer

Ephesians 3:19

HOW TO STAY AT PEACE

There are some things I wish I could change
But, it's not in my power to do
If I could throw a fit and make some things quit
Then I might throw more than a few
Some problems linger too long, It just seems wrong
That answers can't more quickly be found
God says come to Him, He will teach you to swim
But, sometimes the floods try, my soul to drown
Problems aren't so bad when one at a time I have had
But, they are coming in multitudes all the time
I really try to pray but don't quite know what to say
For my words don't seem worth a dime
But, I do find God's mercy is mine
For He keeps me standing tall
He says I can Yield to Him and be filled
I just have to surrender it all
He does give real peace, His mercies never cease
He really pours it all into me
I have truly found He doesn't like a frown
A smile on my face He wants to see
His comfort is real, His peace I can feel
He really will walk me right through
His word has all the power for every day and hour
What He says He expects me to do
He says His burden is light, I walk by faith and not sight
His promises will never ever dim
God promises His grace can be seen on my face
If I just give it all to Him

John 16:33

VALUE OF EXPERIENCE

I like to take some experience in my life
That my God has brought me through
To help someone along the way
So they will know what they can do
To make it through the problem
Whatever it may be
Helping them to understand
The lessons that my God has taught to me
It is a wonderful thing
When someone will do the same in return
Using their experience in the same manner
To share with me what they did learn
That is one thing that God makes so awesome
to allow us to share in lessons so strong
Helping us to avoid really bad mistakes
to help make right things so wrong
We are really blessed to have examples
Of how God loves us so much
that we can share in all of life's treasures
Knowing it is blessed by His special touch

Hebrews 3:13

Soaring to God

There are absolutely
Not enough words to describe
What a great God I see
When He rushes to pick me up
And gives His grace to me
I have learned to trust Him so much
Words cannot describe how I feel
I never knew a love so great
So marvelous and so real
Many hard times He has brought me through
I thought at times my heart would burst
His faithfulness in my hardest pain
Was His love teaching me to trust
I have always wanted someone like Him
Someone I could tell my all
He is even better than I ever hoped
He always catches me no matter how far I fall
He loves me so much He has planned my life
To bring peace to me and glory to Him
Walking ahead preparing my way
Light my path that never grows dim
I know for certain Whatever valley I face
I can trust Him as He takes me through
Raising me up on wings as of Eagles
Soaring to Him through skies of blue

James 4:10

I Now Can See

Until you come to the place
It's just you and God's grace
You will never fully understand His sacrifice

When you can't go one step farther
And you can depend on no other
Only then will you see He paid a great price

What a Savior Jesus is
I now can see His brokenness
I know that for me He has turned the tide

What forgiveness He does send
When my attitude does offend
I see the blood flow from His side

He was bruised and He was broken
the world rejected the Cross as a token
Of the brokenness He suffered for our sin

But, His sacrifice was made
Salvations plan was forever laid
He freely made it for all men

Luke 24:38-39

GOD DON'T DO ANXIOUS

Don't be anxious, don't worry or fret
God is still working, He's not finished yet
He very profoundly does all things right
Time is no bother; He's up all night
He works in a way we cannot see how
That's why we are so anxious, we want it now
He has His own plans, doesn't ask our advice
Let Him do it His way, don't make Him ask twice
If we could be like Him, do like He does
We would be more like the Father, just like Jesus was
Everything has a time and a place you know
God works fast and sometimes He is slow
It's up to Him to send our breakthrough
He is the One that knows what to do
The next time you are anxious take a little test
Quit your worrying, try a little rest
Give it up to Jesus and take time to be still
You will find anxiety doesn't fit in His will

Romans 5:3-5

My Morning With My Creator

When I arise each morning
No matter how bad a night
Excitement comes for experiencing the day
Because God makes all things "right"
It's a joy to face the morning
Knowing that God is in control
Everything that comes my way today
Will be for the good of my soul
My soul cries out to the Father
What a wonderful creation You have made
All You have in store for me today
Keeps me committed not to trade
What I Want and What I desire
Through my eyes may not be good for me
Keep me focused on Your will today
That will keep enjoyment in my day so free
You are my life, my hope for today
Let Your life show forth in me
When I arise again in the morning
My Creator will be ALL I see

Ecc 12:1

REST FOR THE WEARY

When comes the promised rest
Over the things of which I have no control
Over endless barrages of problems
That come to torment my soul
They don't come one at a time anymore
But, regularly in twos and threes
They keep buzzing around my head
Like a continual swarm of bees
But, God is the mighty beekeeper
He knows just how to handle the swarm
He gives me peace that passes understanding
And promises to keep me from harm
Why would I not trust Him
And why would I not know true rest
For God has promised in Jesus the Beloved
He will always give me His best

Matthew 11:28

CHRISTMAS WISHES

If I could make a Christmas wish
And knew it would come true
It would involve a lot of people
And I hope that one wish would do
I have never seen so much trouble
That just seems to never cease
That one wish would be for all those people
To find God's unsurpassed peace
It seems that one can stand any problem
If that peace is planted inside
For in the time that trouble so abounds
There is no desire to run and hide
We are living in a lot of destruction
Caused by nature, storms and war
Fear and what ifs are tormenting people
Trying to find the answer to what for?
Christmas cards say "Joy to the World"
And "Peace for the coming new year"
But, joy and peace will only come
If this message will calm your fear
Jesus came to bring His peace
On that wonderful Christmas Day
Then when He went back to Heaven
He said that His peace would stay
Wonderful peace that only He can give
It will bring us calm in any storm
Our faith in Him and resting in that peace
Will keep us from setting off an alarm
So, my Christmas wish for the season
Is for all who need God's peace
To go to the reason for the season
For He will make sure it will never cease

John 17:25-26

ONE OF GOD'S BLESSED DAYS

I just can't get over God's power last night
And I don't ever really want to
He kept waking me out of my sleep
Saying, "I just want to talk to you"
"There is someone else that you love
that needs to feel what you feel tonight
I just want you to pray for her
I will see that everything is alright"
At first I felt some fear creep up
That was evil trying this moment to make
I prayed for this one I love intensely
Feeling like at that moment she too, was awake
Then, God began to let me see some things
How the devil was planning his attack
I simply ask God to hug her like He did me
Making sure He covered her back
God wants us to believe what He says
We have to know of how He is aware
Of all that we can possibly go through
His presence is what gives us power to share
We have to believe His power is available
That it is ready any fear to calm
To find how willing He is to share with us
Reach for His hand, feel of His palm

John 20:27

BELIEVE IT OR NOT

God gives us plenty to believe
His Word is blessed with His advice
We will not find it in just one scripture
He knows we would need to see it twice
We really have a hard time believing
All the things that God has said
If we fail to hide it in our heart
Reasoning its meaning in our head
God meant just what He said
Every page is ours for a guide
To believe or not to believe
Depends on where you want to abide
In His love and in His power
Or let the world rip you apart
Believe it and live it just as He says
Give Him the throne of your heart
Believe it every minute, every day
It stands forever true
It's not here today and gone tomorrow
Like our believing will sometimes do
We have to stand like God says
His Word is faithful eternally
Believe it and live it like you believe
His Word in action you then will see

Romans 10:9

COST OF THINGS

It never ceases to amaze me
At all the things that can come from hell
To try to convince you you're losing
And life just isn't treating you very well
It can seem like it's all over
That you're on the losing end
That you have been sorely betrayed
By the very one that you called friend
All the things you desire that are good
Seem to keep escaping your grasp
But, you remember your Heavenly Father
Warns about holding onto what don't last
Things are just one of the ways
That evil has to keep us in his hold
He creates in us an overwhelmming desire
For more money, silver and gold
It is not worth what it will cost
To have all these things in control
For in the end the very things
Held so dear will cost your soul
Peace from God is one great treasure
That the world's money cannot buy
There is always an empty spot
Only God can fill no matter how you try
Fill your life with goodness and love
Let go your grasp on the wrong things
Victory will be yours and there will be no defeat
Over anything from hell that evil brings

Luke 15:13

WHICH THOUGHTS DO MATTER

When you get up with so many thoughts
You can't seem to sort them all out
You know there are some that need to be gone
Especially those dealing with doubt
Good thoughts have a hard time staying
When confusion comes from having so many
The evil one will see to it through the day
That you have bad ones more than plenty
The bad ones have got to cease
And they will if you let your thoughts stay
Upward toward our Heavenly Father
Continually praise Him through the day
Come to The Father with a heart full of worship
Trust Him through any kind of day
When worshipping thoughts fill your heart
You won't listen to what bad thoughts say
Good will always win over evil
But, evil will always declares he wins
Worship and praise sent directly to Heaven
Wiil counteract everything evil sends
Start your day with worship to the Father
As soon as you waken in the bed
That will start your day well
Preventing bad thoughts fom filling your head

Phillipians 4:8

A Beautiful Purpose

My life has a purpose, God has an awesome plan
A fulfilling of my being that cannot be changed by man
He has called me out, He has called me from my sin
He has promised me courage, His Spirit is alive within
His strength He has given, Where He needs me to stand
He has written my name in the palm of His hand
He designed me for His purpose, His purpose will endure
He will walk with me always, Of this I know I can be sure

He gave me the power of His blood that He shed
Every drop that left His body as thorns pierced through His head
He gave me a brand new life Just as sure as He came from the grave
Death had tried to destroy Him, but, He would not be death's slave
He is alive in me, He stirs my soul to praise
Dear God let your will be accomplished as I live my allotted days

I have no need of fearing what it is He asks of me
This purpose was set in motion when He allowed my eyes to see
Where it is He brought me from, And where it is I go to
Lord don't listen to my excuses when my purpose You bring into view
Let me walk where You beckon, Let me speak what You give
Let me stand in Your wisdom to fulfill the reason that I live
Help me not to falter as to You my life I give
As your will is finished in my life I'll know I was taught to live

John 12:27

HOW LONG TO GIVE IT?

God says we can cast all our care
On Him for His shoulders are able to bear
Any burden of any size that we bring to Him

He tells us not to worry about
Anything that comes to us and brings doubt
For His Word is proof His promises do not dim

How long can we cast it on Him you ask
How long can He handle the unthinkable task
Of dealing with all the world's problems untold

Mine seem like enough with which to deal
Taking on the whole world seems so unreal
But, He has said the whole world His hands do hold

He will tote the load for all time and ever
If we don't get to thinking that we are so clever
That we have figured our own way to work it out

He doesn't like for us to play give and take
He takes on a lifetime of cares for our sake
For He can defeat the enemy with just a shout

If we take it to God and leave it there
Forever He frees us from the burden of care
Leaving me to live in continual worship and praise

Our time can be spent in energy strong
Singing God's glorious victory song
Giving us wonderful, continual, carefree days

John 7:6

ANSWERS

You can have medicine in a bottle
The advertisement says it never fails
But, if you don't take the medicine
You surely will maintain your ails

You can have direction in detail
To any place in the world you want to go
But, if you don't put them into use
Being lost is probably all you will know

Any professional person in the world
Can hand you "professional" advice
But, if you decide you know more than them
You will discard it never thinking twice

God says He has everything you need
Every direction you need enclosed in His Word
But, if you never pick it up and discover it
Then it's just as though you never heard

Man shall not live by bread alone
Bread can very quickly become stale
If you live and eat and breathe all God says
Then daily you will feast very well

Psalms 119:11

YOUR SPECIAL DAY

Today is your day
God has it all in a plan
He wants your day to be special
He will do everything He can
To make it enjoyable
From beginning to end
Because He loves you so much
Because He is such a wonderful friend
He wants you to have a day
That is free from worry and care
He will take care of all your fear
If you will just remember He is there
He would love to see you enjoy His creation
The grass, the sky and all the trees
He would love to see you smile at life
Sit in the park and enjoy the breeze
Get a glass of cold lemonade
Sit in the shade and watch the Son
Every way you can possibly turn and look
You will see what God has done
It is your choice for twenty-four hours
To live in peace or in despair
God has this wonderful day planned
Every minute with you to share
He will not stay around your misery
So give it up and laugh a while
When you see how special He has made your day
You will spend it all with a smile

Ecc 3:2

MIRACLES OF PRAISE

We all need to learn this secret
If we want to experience better days
No matter how bad the circumstances look
Just begin to send God some praise
He says to seek Him and His righteousness
These other thing fall into place
For when He is first in our thoughts
"Other things" are covered by His grace
Just praise Him for who He is
Praise Him that He is in control
Send Him praise grand and glorious
For being the protector of your soul
Praise Him for meeting your needs
As only your Heavenly Father can
He thinks in ways that are "supernatural"
Never able to be matched by man
Praise warms the heart of our God
Causing Him, our circumstances to tend
How fast He works; I sometimes believe
Depends on how much praise to Him we send
So, if your joy is not up to par
If you want a change in your days
Take time to worship your Heavenly Father, God
Flood His throne with some heartfelt praise

Psalms 147:1

STINKY ATTITUDES

God has proven so many times
That His Word is true
We are believing in our own life
For things He has promised to do
The waiting can be very tedious
If the time factor seems far too long
We can become somewhat frustrated
Thinking He's working it out all wrong
We do not like to be told to wait
But, sometime wait we must
The time it takes to pull things together
Is the time God uses to teach us to trust
When more than one person is involved
In whatever problem God is walking us through
Then that person has to be dealt with also
For the final result God will present to you
God will work on your attitude
More than any other problem you've got
For attitude is one of the worst factors
Making you focus on what is not
You must always remember God has said
He will work all things for our good
We may have problems seeing the answer
Because of our own "stinky attitude"

Romans 5:1

WORRY HAS NO ANSWERS

If you really want an answer
To a problem so great on your mind
You must let God take control
Slow your thinking down and find
When you are chasing thoughts so fast
That your head is in a spin
God can't help you out if
He can't find a place to get in
Don't you see there is a problem
When you let your mind get so confused
Satan almost had you going
He knows how to make you feel abused
God is standing by so quietly
Whispering "Hold on child, I am near"
If you don't stop those gears from turning
The noise of your thoughts won't let you hear
I could sound like claps of thunder
But, unless you quiet down and chill
You will wear yourself out with worry
And not have an answer still!

Matthew 6:27

THE THREAT OF A STORM

We all dread it when storm clouds appear
Threatening a mass of destruction to send
Whether it's main force of fear
Comes from the lightning, rain or wind
Rain can drown a lot of dreams
Or it's rivers can wash them away
The wind can blow them right from your mind
Or lightning can "burn" them up today
There is not a way to avoid a storm
Besides we are not the one in control
Too many factors are involved in the forces
That cause any storm to unfold
Storms always seem to cause great fear
The severity of the storm we don't always know
But, God loves it when we trust in Him
That trust not allowing any fear to show
When the horizon of life reveals signs of a storm
It looks like great damage may be done
Remember that the one in real control
Can return the sunshine after it's gone
When a storm comes in your life
That threatens to destroy your dreams
Remember if Jesus is guiding your footsteps
No storm has the power it seems

I Peter 4:12

God has Fog Vision

It's a really good thing
God sees through the fog in my head today
All the thoughts and feelings that could ruin my morning
I need to let go and usher them to God His way
I think I forgot to let go of anger last night
This morning physically I don't feel too good
With negative self-pity thoughts compounding it all
Nothing about this day will go like it should
I need to focus on some thankfulness
Send God some worship and praise
Choose to have some really good thoughts
Change the evil ones plans for my days
It's not worth the way I feel
To let my day get in such a mess
If I will give it all up to God
The way it ends, I won't have to guess

II Timothy 1:7

BRINGING SCATTERED THOUGHTS TOGETHER

This is one of those times at night
That I feel like I really want to write
But. there seems to be too much on my mind

All my thoughts seem to have scattered
Like not one particular thing mattered
But, I know God's peace I surely will find

The day has been truly blessed
In more ways than I could have guessed
I have shared some things I know only God could have done

Some other things have tried to become a bother
But, I turned them over to the Father
That kept me from wanting to turn and run

He is as faithful as His Word has said
I find myself discovering as I have just this week read
God has truly made the way for me to be free

He has made me dead to sin
Through His Son He causes me to live again
Sin no longer has dominion over me

I don't have to sin to receive His grace
He gave it from the cross hanging in my place
What freedom from His own death He gave

He arose after gaining death's keys to hell
What a privilege to be able to tell
He is alive but my sin remains in the grave

Revelation 1:18

COST OF STANDING

I realize more than ever
There is a cost to stand for what is right
in certain situations you will find
That you must stand up and fight
Words can be your weapon
But, they must use wisdom well
A war fought without wise counsel
will not ring Liberty's bell
God is the greatest giver of wisdom
He understands how the war can be won
He knows how to defend the truth
For without truth it can't be done
Life demands that you have to stand
Where others may not have stood before
But, you have to take the chance
Others will join to help win this war
We cannot live in fear of defeat
Victory won't prevail if we run
God will help us in the battle
We will never have to stand alone
He gives us the courage we need
When we obey all His command
The cost will never be unpayable
If it is in Him that we stand

Acts 7:59

Confidence or Confusion

God is not the author of confusion
Then why do I feel so confused today?
Since I got out of bed this morning
Confusion of old problems has tried to rule my day
I have fought the battle against it
Confident that my God has His reasons
Teaching me not to live by my feelings
They can change as surely as the seasons
Confusion can only capture my thoughts
If my thoughts don't stay in God's control
I will praise Him in spite of the assault
Trusting Him to keep me confident and bold
Those things that try to make me worry
Are best ignored and left in God's plan
I will focus my thoughts on His promises
And my name being written in the palm of His hand
I really have no reason to feel confused
For God has been with me for so long
If the evil one tries to sidetrack me
Then I just continue with a "praise my God song"
Peace and contentment are great side effects
Of walking with God in every day I face
He will put an end to any temporary confusion
Pouring out buckets of His marvelous grace
God has so wisely prepared
His ways to deliver me today
There is no confusion in the way He works
I just confidently follow Him in His way

Hebrews 3:6

GOD'S WAYS ARE HIS OWN

God has some really unique ways
To allow you to find a value for life
You can let Him lead you to them
Or live a lot of years in total strife
He wants us to live in His peace
But, His peace we cannot find
If we don't allow Him to work in us
For His peace is of a special kind
God's peace can conquer all fears
There is not a reason for us to be afraid
For in Him we have all things that we need
To walk in the path that He has made
His peace gives us all His courage
To boldly declare wherein we stand
He takes away all thoughts of dread
He overshadows us with His mighty hand
Jesus had the kind of peace God gives
He said that same peace for us is left behind
He went to His Father after His work was finished
He leads us in ways that peace to find
When all our work is finished
God's peace will have accomplished its job here
He expects us to enter Heaven with a shout
For His wonderful peace has replaced our fear

Isaiah 43:1

LEARNING TIMES

God always has a time of learning
When He wants His children to know
That He really does keep His promises
His unending goodness He wants to show
He teaches us in the way He chooses
For He alone knows just what it will be
That will cause us to focus our attention on Him
Opening our eyes so that we may see
He really does have our best interest at heart
He wants us to know His will at best
There is nothing He will let us walk through alone
Only He is able to give us peace and rest
His lessons are not hard if we listen
For His peace is what always gets us through
Our ears will hear His still small voice
If we are willing His will to do
God really loves us just as we are
He always has and always will
But, He is not willing for us to stay unlearned
That's why the lessons are coming still

Psalms 25:12

SING THE RIGHT SONG

What kind of song are you singing?
Joy, Sorrow or Despair
Oh, Woe is me, I can't make it
Does God really care?
What am I going to do?
How will I get by?
Can anyone feel my pain?
Anyone care if I cry?
Who wrote the words to your song?
The words are not written right
Your song will tell the world
If you live by faith or by sight
The kind of song that you sing
Should tell of the giver of peace
The Hope of all Heaven
Giver of love and blessings that never cease
He is our victor, winner of wars
He is our rampart, our tower so strong
He is the rock on which we can stand
Giver of the words to our song
He is our safe hiding place
He is our sword and shield
He is the giver of our boldness
The one to whom we yield
He is the pilot of our ship
He is the one in control
He is the safe keeper of all we are
He is Savior of our soul
Get that heart song flowing
Sing it to God night and day
When the words remind you of God
Your song will never go away

James 5:13

THE POWERFUL BREATH OF GOD

The power of God overwhelms me
Like a breath I cannot take
it holds me in its grip for a moment
Makes me wonder if I am awake

My senses are so open and filled
With this awesome presence around
I cannot find a word that is fitting
So, I inhale it without a sound

It fills my brain with worship
To the God of Heaven I call King
My heart explodes with total amazement
At the song I want to sing

The song I hear is but two words
They are anything but dim
I want them to ring forever and a day
Two words, simply, Exalt Him

My God is to be exalted
Through the earth let it go like a wind
Let my mouth start the proclamation
Exalt Him, Exalt Him! I will send

He deserves all praise and honor
His breath penetrates into our soul
As it flows through the earth back and forth
It speaks power to us untold

Isaiah 2:10

WEIGHT OF THE CROSS

There is a cross
For all of us to bear
It's not a heavy burden
If we live in God's care
Jesus bore the heavy one
Where he died for our sin
My cross is nothing
Compared to the one where He has been

My cross is nothing
Compared to the one of Heaven's Lamb
It doesn't matter
Who the world thinks I am
I want to be a vessel
That the world can see
leaving behind God's directions
That lead to Calvary

The weight of my cross
Will only drain my strength from me
If I try to carry it alone
And don't stay on my knees
Jesus carried His alone
But, He has promised that He would
Carry mine for me
If I love Him like I should

Galations 6:14

WHEN GOD SPEAKS

When God says, He will
Just sit back and watch Him go
He will work in such a way
That you will have to know
It is HIM

His way to work
He will have to choose
If He has to work your way
Chances are you will lose
Let HIM

God's plans are divine
Yours will not work out
Believe in Him and receive
There's no room for doubt
Believe HIM

Miracles do still happen
We're around them everyday
Whether you actually see them or not
Depends on looking His way
See HIM

God says--Means He does
God says He is--not He was
He is always working for us
He is just looking for our trust
Show HIM

Johsua 1:9

Angels are Here

There is no doubt an angel is about
Sometimes you hear
The rustle of their wings'

In the middle of the night filled with a fright
Sometimes you hear
When their chorus sings

When a smile comes around to replace a worn frown
Sometimes you have to hear
It's an angel's giggle

When you are all worn out cannot move without a doubt
Sometimes you have to hear
Just give a little angel wiggle

When you help a friend who really needs to mend
Sometimes you hear
Go girl that's the way

When you need a shove very gently from above
Sometimes you hear
Angels wings bringing songs
Angels giggling and wiggling
Cheering on your every day

Psalms 34:7 Matthew 26:53

GOD LOVES RELATIONSHIP

No need to write today
I need to be still
Be aware of God's presence
Need to walk in His will

Even writing can distract me
When I should be in prayer
But, I know a thought is pressing
I need to write while it's there

God's presence is much more needed
Than words on paper I write
It's God's strength and power I need
When the storms blow in the night

I have to find a balance
Between words on paper and prayer
For the words God wants on paper
He will make sure they are there

The words all saved on paper
Are reminders to encourage me
But, relationship in God's presence
Is what keeps me safe and free

Mark 10:14

ABOUT THE AUTHOR

Ruby Harris was born in Vincent Alabama. She lived in Dunnavant, Alabama with her husband Ollie and four daughters before moving to Leeds and is now living in Locust Fork, Alabama.

She and Ollie will be married fifty-one years next month and along with the four daughters have six grandchildren and two great grandchildren.

She began writing in 1984.

Printed in the United States
By Bookmasters